7 Steps To A Lean Business

Make your business stand out from the rest

Jason Tisbury

7 Steps To A Lean Business
March 2010
First Edition

www.lulu.com

ISBN: 978-1-4457-6871-7

"It is not the strongest of the species that survive, nor the most intelligent, but the one most responsive to change."

<u>Charles Darwin</u>

7 Steps To A Lean Business

Foreword

So you want to create a lean organisation? Whether you have experienced the benefits of lean or are a complete novice this book can help you along the journey.

Many people shy away from attempting the transformation to a lean organisation as it is often regarded as too difficult to achieve or the benefits too small. This is due largely to much of the available information showing the journey as difficult, often with limited results.

Well I'm here to show you how anybody can create a lean organisation with world class results in 7 simple (I purposely chose not to use the word 'easy' as the journey will be anything but easy) steps. None of this information is new, in fact much of it many decades old. However dated the information may appear, its relevance has not diminished and is just as pertinent today as it was in Japan 60 years ago.

I challenge all business owners and managers to commence the journey towards a lean organisation regardless of the current business, economic or political situation. The time is never 'the right time' just as it is always 'the right time'. Don't wait until tomorrow.

Most readers will have heard of lean through the common term 'Lean Manufacturing'. As anyone who has ever attempted to implement lean will understand, the journey toward lean cannot be limited to the manufacturing processes of an organisation but must reach out to the many other processes of the business in order work effectively.

For the examples in this book I will be using a biscuit factory called 'A. Cookie Company" or ACC. This is a fictitious company and any similarity to an actual biscuit factory is to be regarded as pure coincidence.

For ease of understanding most of the examples within this book are based on the "shop floor". This is because I am expecting most readers to commence their lean journey through the manufacturing processes. All of these tools and concepts can be effectively applied to business systems will a little imagination.

If asked to state "what is lean?" in a single sentence, the answer would be "A systematic process of eliminating the waste from a business to enable the business to reach its ultimate goals."

History Of Lean

So where does the lean story begin? Many people will think of Japan and more specifically Toyota when discussing the history of lean, however it all began long before Toyota was even a company.

One of the traits of human beings that make us stand above all other animals is our desire to be better. What other animals can lay claim to innovation and ingenuity? With this in mind everything we can learn in lean is actually an extension of what is already hardwired into us as a species.

But I feel I have digressed. If we look at the world of manufacturing after the industrial revolution we can see certain points in history that have created a trend.

In the 19th century Benjamin Franklin wrote a number of examples of lean statements. In Poor Richard's Almanac, Franklin discussed how reducing costs could be more profitable than increasing sales. Later in The Way to Wealth discusses the evils of excess inventory with this statement *"You call them goods; but, if you do not take care, they will prove evils to some of you. You expect they will be sold cheap, and, perhaps, they may [be bought] for less than they cost; but, if you have no occasion for them, they must be dear to you. Remember what Poor Richard says, 'Buy what thou hast no need of, and ere long thou shalt sell thy necessaries.'*

In another place he says, 'Many have been ruined by buying good penny worths'."

Frederick Winslow Taylor released his book "Principles of Scientific Management" in 1911. This book discussed breakthrough concepts such as; Standardisation, Best Practice and employee suggestion programs.

Henry Ford was the first true exponent of mass lean production. The drawback of Fords system however was the lack of versatility within the processes. The Ford Production System (FPS) worked extremely well in a stable environment where demand was constant and product variation low or nil. However in a world where customers do not always want their car in black the systems setup by Ford are not as effective. As the FPS relied heavily on parts standardisation, with parts manufactured within upper and lower tolerances allowing for interchangeability.

After WW2 W. Edwards Deming introduced these principles to Japan and specifically to Toyota. Now, Toyota had already been working on improving their own manufacturing efforts for many years with Sakichi Toyoda introducing Jidoka in the early 1900's in the textile factory. Kiichiro Toyoda later realised the waste involved in reworking the cast cylinder heads and went on to develop kaizen or continuous improvement.

The coming together of these two streams of work has developed what we know today as "Lean Manufacturing". Undoubtedly, the best proponent of this over the years has been Toyota, hence the commonly used terms from the Toyota Production System or TPS.

Toyota has also added an almost intangible twist to lean in their philosophy of The Toyota Way. This is where many other companies fail in their quest for a lean business. Lean has to be more than just a production tool and if it is used as a business philosophy or strategy the full benefits of lean can be found.

Lean is not a tool but is a business strategy.

The decision to go lean

As the saying goes 'The first step is the hardest', this is the most difficult of the seven steps. Not difficult because of the work involved but difficult because of the importance of the decision.

The decision to create a lean organisation cannot be taken lightly; the journey will be a long and often painful one. However, the journey will be just as rewarding if the decision to become lean has been made for the right reasons.

It is important that you have all of the facts before making this decision. Detailed below are some of the benefits of a lean organisation, these are followed by some of the common misconceptions or misuses of lean tools.

Benefits:

First some intangible benefits;
Happier employees
Safer work conditions
Increased employee loyalty
Increased customer satisfaction
Reduced quality issues

Now for the tangible benefit;
Increased profits through;
    Increased productivity

Inventory reduction
Lead time reduction
Reduced overheads

Obviously I have listed the intangible benefits before the tangible for a reason, right? Of course I have. The reason is simple, but is the biggest reason why most companies fail in their attempts to become a lean organisation.

If a business decides to become a lean organisation and the core reason behind their decision is to reach the tangible benefits they will most likely fail.

If a business decides to become a lean organisation to reach both the tangible and the intangible benefits they have a good chance of success.

If a business decides to become a lean organisation to reach the intangible benefits they are likely to succeed.

Of course these are not the guaranteed outcomes; however, through observations of the most successful organisations around the world, it is an obvious conclusion. You see, all of these organisations are obviously in business to make a profit, however when you look at the operational goals and objectives, the profit is often not amongst them. Instead, the objectives and goals are largely centred on the intangibles.

If a business is directed effectively and focuses on smart, intangible high level goals as well as an effective "ground level" measurement system then successful lean transformation is highly likely.

5S

The 5S's of Sort, Set in order, Shine, Standardise and Sustain are another one of the tools that form a part of TPS. In the examples from Toyota, 5S forms the foundation of the house with the other tools forming the building. I like to look at 5S as the RIO bar reinforcement mesh that is used in the concrete to provide structure to the foundations. The reason for 5S to form the foundation is more than a play on words. 5S truly is the foundation for all other tools – including lean – to be sustainable.

I have unfortunately seen many years of continuous improvement work fall down just as continuously due largely to the lack of 5S in the organisation. The backwards step usually shows up when production increases as the panic sets in and fire fighting becomes the norm again. Things that were working well when business was constant suddenly become more difficult to maintain. It only takes a single instance of the process not being followed for the bad habits to re-emerge.

There are other causes of course. One of the major factors causing fall back is the lack of commitment at the senior level of the organisation. Often it is this level of employees that make the first "short cuts" to the processes. These short cuts almost ensure that the downstream employees will make more short cuts, and the cycle goes on until the business is back to where it started.

There are other reasons other than senior management commitment that contribute to improvements dropping off. One of these is the lack of an effective 5S program. I stress "effective" here because any system that is not effective might as well not be in place at all. In fact you may be better off with no system at all than a system that is not effective. With no system in place you at least know where the system is currently at, whereas with a system that lacks effectiveness the business can be in a worse situation than it believes.

With an effective 5S program in place the first steps towards sustainable improvements is already in place.

BUT WHAT IS AN EFFECTIVE 5S SYSTEM?

Most of the readers of this book should already have an understanding of what 5S is, however I will give a short overview for any new readers. For an in-depth look at 5S and how to implement an effective system you can read my book "Effective 5S in Your Organisation".

5S originally only had 4 steps and the fifth step was added when transferred from Japan (predominantly Toyota) to western cultures. The S's are reviewed below.

1. Sort – The first S is to sort what is needed and more importantly what is not needed in the work area. A red tag activity is usually held to remove all of the unwanted items. These are located elsewhere until their disposition can be confirmed.
2. Set In Order – This S looks to put everything that should be in the work area in the right locations. The location of items needs to be in relationship to the frequency of use – high frequency items are located close to the operators and low frequency items located further away. These locations need to be identified clearly.
3. Shine – This one is simple. Clean everything – even the areas that wouldn't normally be cleaned.
4. Standardise. Make the new look the new standard. Take a photo and place it on the visual board. If you have a before and after comparison only display it for a short period of time before it is removed. The new standard becomes the basis for the fifth S.
5. Sustain. This fifth S was not originally used by the Japanese, it was added by western cultures because sustaining is not necessarily implied by standardise as it is in Japanese culture.

As part of sustain you will develop the following documents:
- 5S checklist
- 5S audit sheet
- 5S requirement sheet

- Layered audit sheet

5S CHECKLIST

This is a list of key characteristics that have been identified during the standardise step. This checklist can be a daily, weekly or monthly sheet; however it should be performed daily.

The list will include items such as; Raw material within designated area, Bins emptied, Aisles and walkways clear, Cleaning station stocked etc.

5S AUDIT SHEET

The audit sheet is a scorecard that is used to measure the effectiveness of the 5S system by the area leader, team leader etc. This is a list of basic 5S requirements that can be scored from one through to five. Usually an audit sheet will have two items for each of the five S's.

Criteria for each score should be outlined on the audit sheet.

5S REQUIREMENTS SHEET

This is a form to be used for recording any tools, infrastructure, actions that may be seen as necessary to the team.

A very common failing in many businesses is the failure to close off requirement items by management. This leads to lower scores in the area, lowers morale and effectively kills off the 5S journey. Even if the item cannot be approved, close it off. Open items on this form are a sue way to fail.

LAYERED AUDIT SHEET

A layered audit is basically a 5S audit trail that begins in the area and works upwards.

1   The daily or weekly audits are conducted by the responsible team members.
2   The team leader will audit at a later date to measure the effectiveness of the team members auditing.
3   The Group leader or manager will audit to measure the effectiveness of the team leaders auditing and on it goes. The higher in the organisation you can go whilst still maintaining adherence to an auditing schedule the better. However, don't try and go too far and find that the schedule cannot be adhered to by the senior management as this failure to audit will promote poor accountability.

Chapter 1

Where do we start?

There a three distinct answers to this simple question. Each of these answers has worked in the past and each of these will work now and in the future. Although many lean fundamentalists and practitioners believe that one of these three is the correct method, I believe that in many instances, internal pressures will not allow an holistic lean approach.

The three options will be discussed in this chapter – the benefits, drawbacks, potential struggles and situational requirements. As the reader, you know how your business operates so are in a better position to determine the best option for your circumstances.

Option 1 – Start at the end

This is the method most widely believed to bring the greatest results.

THE CONCEPT

This journey begins at the end process.

The idea being that if the final process is improved, then deficiencies in earlier processes will be highlighted. This is the best holistic approach and if the journey is followed to fruition will provide the greatest results to the entire business.

BENEFITS
- Provides the best outcome
- Will 'fix' the greatest number of issues
- Provides a logical path
- Creates a need for supplier processes to improve

Imagine the A. Cookie Company (ACC) warehouse, full of pallets and pallets of biscuits waiting to be shipped to wholesalers and distributors. The amount of inventory equates to 3 days of customer requirement. With this amount of inventory the need to improve is difficult to see, let alone justify.

This inventory build up is evident at every processing stage through the factory.

When starting at the end is followed and the warehouse is the first working area to be analysed and improved the results will be immediately obvious to the business. When the 3 days inventory is reduced to less than 1 day the overall lead time is reduced by 2 days, meaning the product is invoiced 2 days earlier than previous. Customers will also benefit from this shorter lead time.

The above benefits are the obvious ones. The hidden benefits can be seen when the inventory reduction in the warehouse creates a shortage in supply. How can a shortage be a benefit? This shortage will create the chaos required to really get the improvement process going as the business will demand the supplying process is able to provide enough product to meet customer demand. When this supplier process is improved and the excess inventory around the process is removed then the next supplier process will be the chaos. This cycle continues over many months until every process in the business is analysed, improved and a new standard is set.

DRAWBACKS

- Progress can be slow
- The chaos that is created can destabilise the business
- The improvements must be sustainable otherwise old practices will be reinstated as the chaos begins

Although the numbers of negatives is low, their impact can be devastating to any lean program.

Back in the ACC factory we have reduce the warehouse inventory from 3 days to less than 1 day. The following week a customer places a larger than ordinary order. Without the stock in the warehouse and with the factory unable to produce the order in time, the business is unable to fulfil the order in time and the customer cancels.

In this situation it is likely that the lean journey will take a hammering and possible demise.

POTENTIAL STRUGGLES

It is common with this method of lean for the team and others in the business to want to jump to the next project too soon. This is due to the chaos created during the improvement process.

REQUIREMENTS

It is imperative that the team implementing lean with this method has the total support of the business. This is especially needed from the senior or executive management.

This support will be necessary to provide stability to the improvement team during times when any negativity is running high.

Option 2 – Start at the beginning

This method is often used by inexperienced lean implementation teams.

THE CONCEPT

This journey begins at the first process.

With this method, the beginning process is worked on first. After improving this process internal pressure will be applied to the following processes to improve and realise the potential benefits.

BENEFITS

- Fast 'visible' benefits
- Follows a logical path

In the ACC factory, the raw materials are delivered to the preparation department. The preparation dept is where the raw materials are mixed together before cutting.

We know that there is 3 days inventory between each process. Suppose that a batch of Product A is incorrectly baked and needs to be remade urgently. With 3 days inventory between each process it is possible that it could take at least this time to respond.

However, if improvements are made to the preparation dept. this responsiveness may be improved significantly.

DRAWBACKS

- It can be difficult to maintain the improvement as the next process is not demanding the improvement
- Chaos is not created by the improvements
- Depending on the businesses culture, management may lose interest once the initial improvements are realised

It is often the case with this strategy for the team to lose sight of their direction so individual, team and departmental plans that all drive toward a common goal is imperative (it is a very good idea for any business to create a process for structured goals and work plans).

POTENTIAL STRUGGLES

As with Option 1, it is important to ensure the improvements are sustainable before moving on to the next project. It cannot be stressed enough how important this is. One of the major reasons that improvements fail is because they have been left in an unsustainable state. If the process can fail, it will.

REQUIREMENTS

A well structured plan is important with this process as the "next" process for improvement will not be as obvious as in Option A. This is due to the lack of chaos caused.

Option 3 – Start at the bottleneck

This process appears to be the easiest. It's easy to see the bottleneck in a factory or warehouse right? Not always. It is a common mistake to identify the wrong bottleneck. It is very important to make all judgements based on data. Good analysis of data is essential when choosing this option.

THE CONCEPT

By beginning the journey at the bottleneck process it is possible to see fast improvements in the business. After improving this bottleneck, the next bottleneck process can be identified and improved. This cycle is continued.

BENEFITS

- Fast visible benefits
- With effective data the pathway to improvements can be clear

Back at the ACC factory the ovens have been identified as the bottleneck. The data indicates that preparation takes 12 minutes to complete while the oven cell takes 18 minutes to complete. This leaves a build up of inventory after the preparation cell.

With some minor improvements to the oven cell this process has been improved to 13 minutes. With this one improvement a 27% increase in output has been realised.

The next bottleneck process is now identified and the cycle continues.

DRAWBACKS

With effective data collection and analysis there are few if any drawbacks to this option. However, this option is the least likely to bring sustained improvements. This is due to the fact that effectively data collection and analysis is not often available, particularly with businesses that are at the earlier stages of lean development.

By identifying a false bottleneck, all of the resources used to implement an improvement will not provide benefits. Moreover, without benefits, the future of lean development may be in question.

POTENTIAL STRUGGLES

The main struggles that will be found by employing this option will likely be the lack of understanding of the importance of good data by the decision makers. Management often underestimate the value of data collection.

REQUIREMENTS

The best way to ensure this option will be effective will be to implement a data management system at least six months prior to commencing the first project.

A Value Stream Map (VSM) is a powerful tool that can be used to determine the bottleneck processes.

The importance of choosing the correct method for your circumstances cannot be stressed strongly enough. The cost of choosing the incorrect method can be much higher than the dollars invested. For this reason, it is well worth investing the resources to correctly selecting the method that best suits your situation.

Lean Requirements

There are a number of core requirements that must be present for any lean journey to be successful. If all of these requirements are not present the journey will not be totally successful, although some successes may be encountered.

It is an unfortunate truth that most lean journeys are unsuccessful in that these requirements are not present. Lean is often seen as a magic wand that can be swished over the organisation and bring about increased profits. Without the right motivations lean will only bring isolated improvements that are unlikely to be sustained.

All of the success stories have one thing in common; the business structure and departmental work plans are linked to the organisations strategic plan.

REQUIREMENT 1 – EXECUTIVE DRIVING FORCE

This is probably the most common failing in organisations attempting a lean journey. Unfortunately executive level management often do not have a thorough understanding of lean and how it works. This means that the resources allocated to achieving lean may be measured incorrectly and short term goals and objectives may interfere with the longer term potential outcomes.

It is essential that the driving force behind the lean journey comes from the executive team otherwise the commitment of the business will be questioned internally. Moreover the lean resources may become used as a cost cutting tool that is used on a whim.

Ideally, the executive team will have lean as a part of a strategic plan. This strategic plan will be followed by all departments of the organisation, with their own plans aligning to achieve the corporate goals.

Often the lean resources are measured by the savings they bring to the company which in itself is fine as there needs to be a cost benefit to the business. However, it is essential that the executive management understand that lean is a journey and that just like taking a plane flight rather than a bus for a long journey is the most effective method you may need to drive a little bit further to get to the airport rather than the bus stop. We should not expect to gain a cost savings from every activity undertaken. These "non cost saving" activities are still value adding because without them the future cost benefits may not be achievable.

This is similar to the value adding, non value adding and incidental work from a value stream map – the value adding portion is when an activity directly impacts positively on the business and its goals.

Incidental work is anything that may not directly impact in the same way but is necessary to achieve a future target or benefit. Non value adding work is where the activity does not impact positively now and will not lead to any impact in the future.

REQUIREMENT 2 – RESOURCES

Many organisations decide to start on the lean journey but do not allocate the resources to make it a success. One person alone cannot change the organisation; however that one person can change it with the right resources in place.

The company structure needs to enable the lean champion to be successful. All managers from middle management up need to have some understanding of lean concepts. Without an understanding of the concepts, the job of the champion will be extremely difficult. For example, imagine trying to explain the benefits of a pull system between two departments over a push system to a group of managers that have never heard of these terms.

In this example the champion will have to explain in detail what these terms mean before the benefits and detailed process can be discussed. The first problem faced will probably be the lack of willingness from the managers to admit they do not know what the terms mean. If the champion assumes that they do know, this discussion will not be effective. If however the champion assumes that the managers do not have prior understanding of the concepts and proceeds to explain them in detail he may be seen as condescending. This is a no win situation for the lean champion.

Another issue regularly seen is when resources are regularly moved from the activities to fill holes in the business. This is obviously disruptive for the activity and the participants but also shows a lack of commitment from the business. This has a huge negative impact on the culture and should be avoided at all costs.

To sum up it is important that the business chooses to undertake the lean transformation for the right reasons. This should be as part of an overall strategic plan and not as a cost reduction exercise. If introduced and followed correctly the outcomes provided by lean systems will change the business in many ways, happier employees, less staff turnover, reduced safety risks, reduced inventory, reduced WIP plus many more. These benefits will all ensure that the operating costs will be reduced more than if the decision is made for a cost reduction outcome only.

Where ever you decide to start the journey it is important to scope the project prior to commencing. By scoping the project you will have a clear understanding of what is to be achieved as well as when the project is finished. The following points should be determined when scoping a project:

1. Sponsor – This is a person who has the authority to direct the participants.
2. Owner – This is the owner of the process and is the person ultimately responsible for completion of the project.
3. Facilitator – Usually a lean black belt, green belt or TPS champion.
4. Scope – Where the project starts and finishes.
5. Objective – What is to be achieved?
6. KPI's – What KPI's are in place to measure the outcome.

Along with these points it is a good idea to include the following:

1. Background – What is currently occurring to identify this as a suitable project?
2. Timeframe – How long is the project expected to take.
3. Costs – Are there any expected capital costs to the business.
4. Expected outcome – How will the process look after the project.

Chapter 2

Genchi Genbutsu

Genchi Genbutsu means to go to the source. This is a Japanese term that has come from Toyota and is an integral part of the Toyota Production System. Put basically it means to go and see the problem for yourself rather than rely on information coming to you.

An example of this is if your car is not running correctly. You could ring up your mechanic and try to explain the sounds, smells, feeling etc but it would be difficult for your mechanic to diagnose the problem correctly – even for a simple issue. However if your mechanic can see, the car and go for a test drive, the problem is easier to diagnose.

The same applies in the workplace. Always see for yourself whenever possible.

Is there a difference between Genchi Genbutsu and Gemba? Gemba refers to the place where the process is performed. A common term is to "walk the Gemba". This means to walk the factory floor in a manufacturing business and is a very valuable tool. Genchi Genbutsu however is a little different

A regular Gemba walk is a must for any leader or manager to understand how their department or business is going. The more regular these walks become the better, as with regularity comes complacency, meaning the workforce will become used to the management being around and you will see the "real" story.

Some of the benefits from regular Gemba walks are:

- Waste identification
- Clear understanding of processes
- Promotes team work between management & workforce
- If problems occur, relationships are already in place between management & workforce

I encourage all managers and owners to take part in Gemba walks regularly.

Now onto Genchi Genbutsu. This is different to a Gemba walk in that it is better NOT to walk. In many of the best lean businesses it is common for a manager to stand and watch a particular operation for many hours.

Unfortunately, most other businesses do not follow the practice to the same extent and this shows in their outcomes.

HOW DO WE GET STARTED?

It is a good idea for Genchi Genbutsu to follow on from some form of problem identification. A very good saying I heard is "what get measured gets managed". This is very true. A system for measuring performance is critical in any business. If you don't know what the problem is, how can you possibly fix it? So, if you do not already have s system in place for measuring the critical processes in your business go and start measuring.

Because this is so important I will spend some time on measurement in this chapter. Measurement should be in place before the decision to go lean is made. However I know that this does not always occur.

What should be measured? Well I cannot tell you what you should measure without seeing your business but a simple rule is that anything that can have a negative impact on the desired outcome should be measured in some way. Why do we measure? We don't measure processes to find out how many products we are making. This alone isn't important. Only measure something that can be compared against a target or goal.

For example, if your customer needs 10 packets of biscuits each day, then you can measure how many packets of these biscuits you make. If you only make 8 each day then you can see that you have a problem that needs fixing. The same measurement can be used for new product development. If your customer requires you to develop their new biscuit in 16 weeks and you take 20 weeks to develop it then you have a problem that needs fixing.

You can see from these examples that measurement systems can be useful, but they can also be cumbersome if used incorrectly. A simple rule is if you measure something and the results can not help identify a problem then you are probably measuring the wrong thing. Don't be scared to change what you are measuring is you aren't getting the outcome you need.

It is a good idea to have a target for all measurements. These targets should be "SMARRT" – Specific, Measurable, Achievable, Realistic, Responsibility, and Time. Without a target the measurement will not identify any problem.

Remember, measurement in business is not to show how good you are – it is to identify where a problem exists.

Now, back to Genchi Genbutsu. In the ACC factory, we have a measurement system in place and this data has highlighted a problem with the rolling machine.

The cutting machine that follows is having to stop and wait for product regularly. This means that the rolling machine is a bottleneck.

We have the data to prove this – problem definition. Now we all know that the next step is to analyse the problem and find the cause – root cause analysis.

There are 3 ways we can do this.
A) Perform root cause analysis as a management team. Without experts from the production area we will likely miss important information and come to the wrong conclusion.
B) Perform root cause analysis with the production experts and rely on them to provide factual, evidential information. Although unintentional, we may get information that is biased or does not take into account all of the variables.
C) Perform root cause analysis with a cross functional team. This will ensure the majority of stakeholders are involved and the decision making process will be both more efficient and more effective.

In many organisations Option C is as far as they would go to ensure the correct problem is identified, analysed and solved. Many other companies go further than this. Even if they don't realise it, they are performing Genchi Genbutsu.

At the ACC factory we have designated a cross functional team to work on the problem – this gives us the same situation as Option C above. However, this team is working on the shop floor to "see" the issue first hand. They are not just walking through the cell or factory, they are walking to the area of concern, in this case the rolling machine.

After arriving at the rolling machine the team stops and watches the process – this includes the process supplier and customer processes. How long should they stand and watch? The answer to this question is simply as long as it takes to understand the process well enough. It is important that everyone in the team has this opportunity, ideally together as a team if possible.

It is a good idea to do this over a number of days. If time is a major problem break it up into ½ hour visits. Remember though, the more time you do this will achieve a couple of positive outcomes.

- Members of the team will have a chance to raise questions for themselves to check on their next visit.
- The operators in this work area will be more open to the audience and the observers will see what really happens.
- This may provide the team an opportunity to observe a number of different products, operators or circumstances.

The team members should be given the opportunity after these sessions to review what they have observed to ensure they get the most from the session.

It is important that every person involved the next step of current state be given the opportunity of following Genchi Genbutsu.

Many managers have difficulty understanding the value of Genchi Genbutsu. They will be the same managers who assign value to the hours worked over the value added. We've all had these managers in the past. Their expectation of the workers is to start early and finish late, regardless of what work there is to do. They will often sit at their desk waiting for everyone to leave even if there is no work to be performed, just so that they can be the last to leave for the day.

These managers need to understand the difference between value and non value work. The very fact that you are reading this book indicates that you are not a manager of this mindset.

If you work in a company where this style of management is in power then the task of implementing lean will be more difficult. This does not mean that it is impossible however. It may take longer (which in itself is a problem with these managers) but slowly get them involved in the process. This may need to be done without them knowing what you are doing. I find a good method is to ask them for their input or help frequently. This tends to stroke their ego whilst getting them involved, be careful not to come across as incompetent of making your own decisions though. This may be a bit of a tight rope walk to get the right balance.

Just remember that even of something you try doesn't work, it isn't a failure – for two reasons. 1. You are closer to a solution that will work. 2. Now you know what doesn't work.

TAKING IT FURTHER

Recently I have tested a theory that I have had for quite some time. I always try to gather a cross functional team into any improvement project or activity, but I often find that those participants that do not work in the problem area either take too long to understand the process being observed or can often say they understand when in fact they do not. This isn't too big of an issue if the problem or process is relatively small, however with a big problem or large process this can be a substantial issue.

My theory was to place the team member in a position to work within the process for a period of time prior to the team coming together. This doesn't necessarily mean working on the tools, it can be as a leader or even in a customer or supplier capacity.

This enables the person to gain an in-depth understanding of the process, the problem and how the effects of the problem.

As I said earlier, this should only be followed for a major project.

Chapter 3

The Current State

This is where the fun begins. Up to this point we have been looking at the benefits that undertaking a lean journey can provide and some of the requirements an organisation should provide in order to get the most from the transition. Now we are about to go into the improvement process.

The basic improvement process developed by Deming is the foundation that should be followed during any improvement project. Plan, Do, Check, Act – PDCA or sometimes referred to as PDSA (the S stands for study rather than act).

The process always begins with planning. This step usually takes up to 2/3 of the project timing. As you read this book you will notice that the 7 steps of this book are based on this cycle. The first two chapters would be included in the Planning stage. This chapter and the next are also both in the planning stage (some parts of chapter 4 are also in the Do stage as will be explained later).

Plan – Analyse what has gone wrong? Find a gap and make a plan to implement countermeasures.

Do – Trial the countermeasure.

Check – Measure the outcomes from the trial to determine the effectiveness.

Act – If the countermeasures provide the desired outcomes – implement on a larger scale and share the lessons learnt. Otherwise develop new countermeasures and return to Do.

This step is also where many of the lean tools come into play. This book is too small to include all of the tools that are available to assist in the measuring and development of the current state, however we will include as many as possible.

We already have an understanding of where the problem is. Now we have to identify what the problem is. A basic process we follow is the use of effective measurement systems to identify gaps. Depending on what stage of the lean journey your organisation is at, different tools will provide the best solutions.

Some of the tools that can be used are outlined below.

VALUE STREAM MAP

A value stream map (VSM) is used to visualise the value adding and non-value adding work performed in a process. Value adding work is basically any process or step that the customer is willing to pay for.

A VSM is useful when looking at the entire process e.g. The manufacturing process.

To begin a VSM the first step is to develop a process map, then the timing studies need to be undertaken for all of the processes (process study). Measurement of the inventory between processes is important to capture.

The process studies are then mapped onto the VSM with the inventory added between processes.

The outcome is a map showing the value added, non-value added and lead time for a product to pass through the system.

Many practitioners steadfastly believe that a VSM (and most other tools) should always be completed by hand to develop a better understanding of the processes being mapped. I understand the thinking behind this however I must admit that I prefer to finish off my work on a computer as I make too many changes as I go.

An example of a Value Stream Map can be found in Appendix 1.1

Once the map is complete it is a relatively easy task to analyse the timings and determine the greatest gains can be made. It is important to mention that before analysing the VSM you should have an idea of what your general problem is – more on this when discussing the future state. As the basic principle of lean manufacturing is to eliminate the "waste" or non value adding activities from a businesses processes the greatest gains can often be found by looking at the inventory or holding areas.

I have used this tool to map out the entire process in the current state before starting any improvement activities. It may be time consuming the first time it is performed as all of the process studies each take time, however the benefits of this work will be gained in the future.

PROCESS MAP

A process map is a flow charting system that is used to visualise the process flow. On paper starting with the first step, write down each step that occurs with in the process.

These maps can range from high level to macro level maps that will detail each movement of the process.

It is a good idea to map out the process from both directions also. I find that by starting at the end step, it is easy to see the previous step. Conversely, by starting at the first step you may see that the process divides at some point. By mapping the process in both directions you will have a more reliable process map.

An example of a process map can be found in Appendix 1.2

PROCESS STUDY

A process study is an in depth analysis of a process. This can be later used in the development of a VSM.

To undertake a process study, it is first necessary to observe the process to gain a thorough understanding of the entire process. This is necessary to ensure that a standard process is able to be measured.

Write down the steps of the process that you want to measure. The more detailed the study then the better analysis can be achieved later. The less detailed the study then the more easily the study can be performed. It is a good idea to begin with less detail until you become more proficient.

Some points to remember:
- Measure 10 consecutive processes
- Record information such as time, date, operators etc
- Perform 3 studies

After the studies are complete the data is collated and transferred to a process chart for further analysis.

An example of a process study can be found in Appendix 1.3

SIPOC

A SIPOC diagram is often used as a starting point for collecting information during a project. SIPOC stands for Supplier, Input, Process, Output, Customer.

As the name suggests this tool is used to identify all of the stakeholders within and external to a process.

Ideally, this would be completed after the process map. At this point, the SIPOC diagram is developed as an extension of the process map. The main difference between the process map and process column of the SIPOC is the level of depth. The SIPOC is intended to be a higher level tool.

The page is divided into five columns. The process steps are entered in the centre column. This is followed by the inputs which are entered to the left of the process. The outputs are then entered to the right of the process. The suppliers of each input is entered in the far left column and finally the customers are entered into the far right column.

It is critical that the SIPOC be completed by a cross functional team. After completion it is also important to share the outcome with the team responsible for the process as well as the critical suppliers and customers. This will ensure the diagram is accurate.

MATERIAL FLOW DIAGRAM

This is often referred to as a spaghetti diagram due to its physical appearance. As the name suggests, this is a diagram used to show the path that the material follows during processing.

It is important to first draw the floor layout as accurately as possible. The start points for the process are indicated with the numeral "1'. There can be multiple starting points for a process as components may combine at a later step.

The flow of the material to the next step is now drawn. As before there may be multiple subsequent steps. The flow must show the actual path of the material and not take any false path. These steps are identified as "2". Continue this until the material diagram is complete.

The tool is helpful in identifying obvious waste in the process. Just as "One piece flow" is the Holy Grail for lean manufacturing, a one direction material flow diagram is the best outcome. Any time the material crosses its own path or backtracks is waste.

An example of a material flow diagram can be found in Appendix 1.4

These tools are very powerful when used to their full potential. The difference between a successful project and an unsuccessful project can often be in the accuracy and relevance of the current state data. A common mistake made by inexperienced lean practitioners is to hurry this stage of the project. It is important that the collection of current state data is complete, accurate and relevant before continuing.

If the data collected is not relevant then it is important to change path and ask a different set of questions. I will spend some time on this subject as it is a critical step. It is good practice to have a measurement and analysis system in place in your business regardless of whether a project is underway or planned.

MEASUREMENT SYSTEMS

Back at ACC factory, suppose we are measuring the output from each work cell and have been doing so for many years. How do we, as managers and leaders, benefit from this measurement? If the answer is little or no benefit, then we are measuring the wrong things.

It is a good idea to introduce multiple measurements for the same work area or machine. Sometimes these measurements may appear to be in conflict with each other, however we often need to do this to show how one failure can have an impact on another area. This will enable us to find the root cause of the problem.

For instance, we are measuring the output from the ovens at the ACC factory. The graphical output from this system is below.

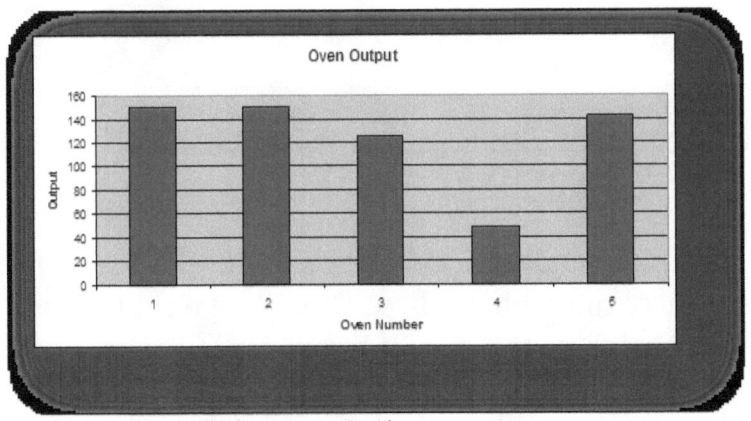

(Diagram 3.1)

Looking at this graph it is obvious that we have less output from oven 4 than the other ovens.

How can we fix this?
Without more information it is not possible to fix this. Unfortunately many businesses spend time and resources doing exactly this. Do we even know if there is a problem or is the problem just assumed?

After looking at the measurement system, some changes have been made in the below graph.

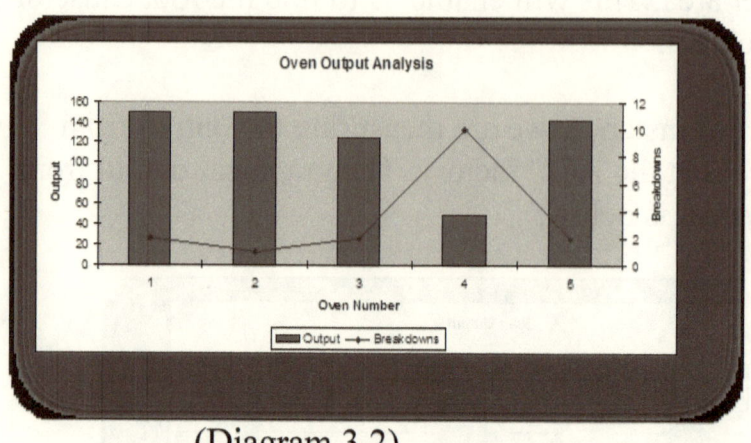

(Diagram 3.2)

By simply adding another axis to the chart we can now see where the problem lies. This is not a root cause but it does enable us to perform a root cause analysis of the problem.

In the first graph the problem could be defined as "Oven number 4 is producing lower output than the other ovens."

In the second graph the problem can now be defined as "Due to excessive breakdowns, oven number 4 is producing lower output than the other ovens."

What is we see a graph like the one below?

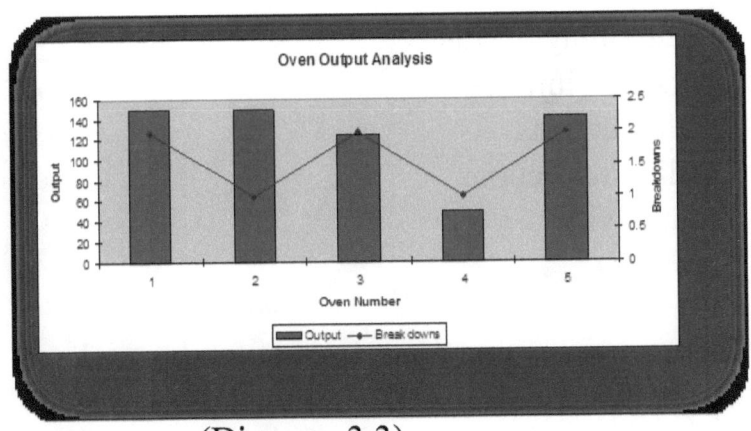

(Diagram 3.3)

This graph is showing that the measurement system in place is not providing us with sufficient information to identify the problem. In this situation we need to try data point to accompany the output.

Some of the key metrics that should be considered include:

- Output
- Breakdowns
- Downtime
  - o Planned
  - o Unplanned
- Uptime
- Machine efficiency
- Changeovers
- Absenteeism
  - o Planned
  - o Unplanned

- Staff training / skills
- Incidents / injuries
- Quality defects
- Quality inspections
- Productivity
- Shortages

There are many more metrics that can be used. The skill of a manager is to know which measurement suits the situation and will provide the best information. This skill can only be learned through practise.

If your business does not already have an <u>effective</u> measurement system in place I highly suggest this be your first step. This is not meant to be a book on culture change, however the introduction of an effective measurement system can be a strong starting place to introduce a culture of accountability into a business.

If you look through the metrics on the preceding page you may notice that some of the items can be regarded as "What" measurements and others as "Why".

If a "what" measurement is used in conjunction with a "why" measurement it is possible to identify where the problem is.

When we go back to graph 3.2 or 3.3 we can see that the "what" is labelled "Output" and the "why" is labelled "breakdown".

As the current state is about identifying where the business is now, it is easy to see why measurement systems and data collection form a major part of this chapter, However, it is not the total picture.

It is critical that the current state information can be expressed in a concise manner. It is great to have a desk full of documents detailing the current state, but if this cannot easily be explained or visualised than what is it worth?

Always maintain a one page document for each project or activity. This document should include but is not limited to:

- Scope – What areas or products does the activity include? What doesn't it include?
- Objectives – Identify the 4 main objectives for the business
- Background – What brought about this activity? What was the driver?
- KPI's – List the 3 or 4 main KPI's to be measured.
- Current state – What are the current measures of the KPI's?
- Future state – What are the expected KPI measurements?
- Plan – How will the future state be achieved?

This document should be reviewed regularly to ensure any amendments to the plan are updated. Share this document with the project team and communicate with the relevant stakeholders.

This brings us to the point of communication. It is during the current state collection stage of the project that employees outside of the project will usually first become aware that a project is taking place. This is poor communication.

Depending on the size and scope of the project, communication needs to be open and upfront to the business. This is particularly true when the business is starting out on the lean journey as it is likely that the workforce will be uneasy with the concepts of change. The earlier these changes are communicated and discussed openly, the better the outcomes will be.

It is important that the concerns of employees are not pushed aside but are listened to and clearly understood by management. If the employees do not feel respected at this early stage then the implementation will likely be met with greater resistance.

Without good, open communication the initial efforts to bring about change will suffer. Almost all managers talk about culture change as if it is some unobtainable dream, this is not the case. If handled correctly the culture can change positively and quickly. It all comes down to a couple of factors.

1   **Communication** – Companies that successfully implement lean (or any other change for that matter) have an effective communication system. This means that each person in the organisation has a level of awareness of issues in line with their role and responsibilities. As companies grow they often forget about the communication channels and the changes they need to keep up with the growth.

2   **Structure** – The organisational structure must support the desired culture change. Most companies define the corporate values, mission and vision and think this will change the culture. If the structure cannot or does not support the vision, then how can the rest of the business be expected to change.

3   Commitment – Commitment to achieving the vision is needed from the executive team. This commitment and drive will filter down through the organisational structure and to the management levels below.

With these 3 factors in place the challenge of changing a company's culture becomes a journey.

Unfortunately, most businesses either do not understand this concept or choose to ignore it.

We'll go back to the current state now. There are some key points to keep in mind when collect and collating information for the current state.

- Things are what they are
  - o This simply means that it is important to report what you see. If the situation is bad, then show it that way. Don't get sucked into sugar coating the truth.
  - o If you miss something, go back and see. It is human nature to "fill in the gaps". This must not occur. It is very common to miss something in the observations especially when you are new to lean.
  - o Don't be scared to question what you observe.
- Gain consensus
  - o This is a must. It is vital that you have the agreement from all stakeholders on the current state before you go to the next step.
- There is no such thing as bad data
  - o The more information you can gather, the better you will be set up for success. This is especially true when starting out on the journey.
  - o If you find you have data that is not helpful, just discard the data and put it

> down to experience. The only thing you
> have lost is your time.
>   o As you gain more experience, you will
>   become better at selecting the right data to
>   collect.

- Take your time to get it right
  - o Do not underestimate how long this step
    can take.
  - o Collecting and collating the information for
    the current state can take up to 60% of the
    project time.
  - o Utilise any existing measurement systems
    before introducing new systems.
- Don't rely on data alone
  - o A picture paints a thousand words, so take
    as many pictures as you can.
  - o With the introduction of digital cameras,
    the life a lean engineer is improved out of
    sight.
  - o Appendix 2 has some great tips on how to
    get the most from your photography.

Chapter 4

To The Future

Welcome to the future! Well we're not there yet, but we are getting there. At least that is the plan right. Talking about plans, if you look at the PDCA cycle above, we are still in the planning stage. As mentioned in the last chapter, the planning stage is often more than half of the project length. In this step we are about to let our imaginations take over and begin planning where we want to be.

In this chapter we will discuss some of the tools that can be useful when designing the future state. I have chosen to use the word "design" to describe this process because the future should be developed from a clean slate just as a new design of any type would be. The basic process followed to design the future state is below in diagram 4.1

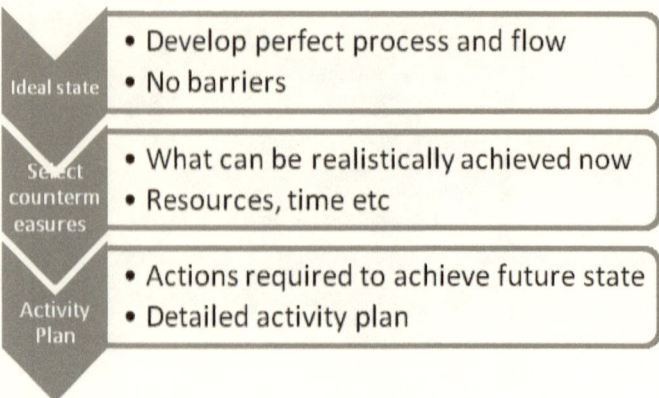

Ideal state
- Develop perfect process and flow
- No barriers

Select countermeasures
- What can be realistically achieved now
- Resources, time etc

Activity Plan
- Actions required to achieve future state
- Detailed activity plan

(Diagram 4.1)

IDEAL STATE

Not all lean practitioners use this step because they see it as waste (which in itself is against lean principles). I see this step as more incidental work rather than waste or non value adding work. You will remember value adding work being discussed briefly, diagram 4.2 shows the relationship between value adding, non value adding and incidental work. Notice that the non value adding work is viewed separately while the value adding and incidental has a closer relationship.

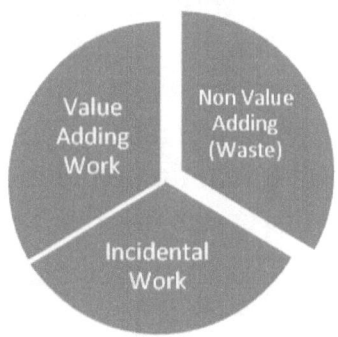

(Diagram 4.2)

Value adding work can be described as any work that is performed that your customer would be happy to pay for. An example may be going to a dentist to have your teeth cleaned.

What are you paying for? To get your teeth cleaned.

Non value adding work is best described as any work that is performed that the customer is NOT willing to pay for. The expense of this work must be consumed by the business.

I'm sure you wouldn't be willing to pay for the dentist the find the correct cleaning bit to complete the task of cleaning your teeth. The fact that he cannot locate his tools is absolute waste as this could easily be eliminated.

Incidental work is any work that must be performed in order to complete the value adding work. Just as non value adding work or waste can be reduced or eliminated, incidental work can also be greatly reduced. It can be difficult to eliminate the incidental work due to the relationship and is usually eliminated by costly process improvements.

Back at the dentist an example of incidental work could be the application of cleaning paste to the cleaning tool. This application is necessary to complete the task so cannot be classified as waste, however it is not the direct reason for your visit to the dentist. This could be reduced in time by relocating the paste dispenser closer and eliminated by purchasing a self pasting cleaning tool – this would cost a great deal so may not be a practical solution.

Now you may be able to understand why I see this step as more incidental work than waste. Without this step of creating an ideal state it can be difficult to create the future state without allowing too many obstacles obscure your view.

The concept of creating an ideal state can described as a dream state as this needs to be developed with no constraints in mind for this reason it can be better performed by people with existing lean experience or people who are adept at free thinking and conceptualisation.

This step is also when some of the tools associated with lean are brought into play. Most of these tools are designed to support and enable Just In Time (JIT) material delivery systems.

JUST IN TIME

The concept of JIT came from a visit to the USA by Taiichi Ohno of Toyota after WW2. It was during this visit that he found the answer to the problems that Toyota was having –low demand after the war did not allow Toyota to benefit from the mass production systems being utilised overseas.

Look at how a supermarket works:
- A product is purchased
- This leaves a space on the shelf
- This space is filled from the warehouse
- This creates a space in the warehouse
- An order is raised to the supplier to fill this space.

Without being aware of it the early supermarkets had developed a new supply chain method that would change the world of manufacturing.

Ohno took this idea back to Japan and Toyota and began implementing what is now labelled Just In Time.

The objective of JIT can be best explained as a method to get the right things, to the right place or person, at the right time, in the right quantity to achieve perfect flow of work while still being flexible enough to allow for changes in demand.

Some of the tools created to assist in implementing JIT are explained below.

PULL SYSTEM

To understand how a pull system differs from a standard push system it is first necessary to understand how a push system works and the impact this has on a business.

The following diagram (Diagram 4.3) depicts a general business that is using employing a push system. Once again the ACC cookie factory is used in the example. This example begins at the flour hopper and continues only to the next value adding process. As this example shows the amount of inventory and waiting time between processes is high. This is a push system of manufacturing; the product is pushed to the next process with no regard as to the current workload of the process.

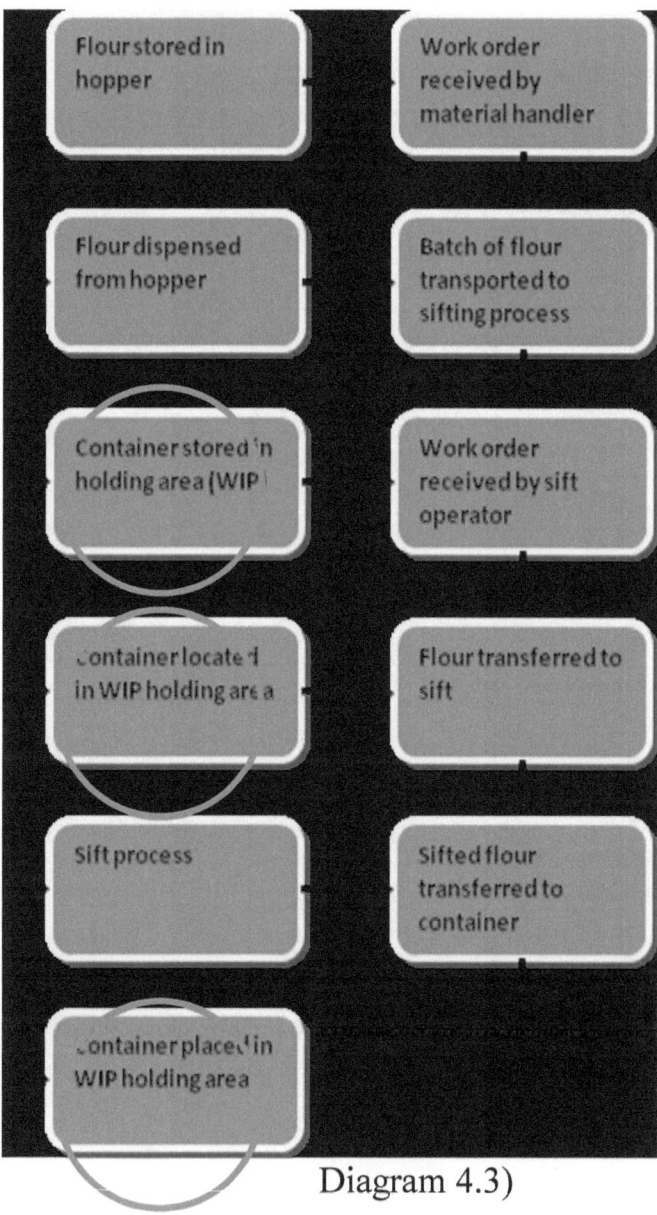

Diagram 4.3)

In this example three of the eleven steps are waste, two are value adding and six are incidental work. This equates to 27% of the process being waste, if we convert this to a VSM the waste is emphasised even more as shown in diagram 4.4 below.

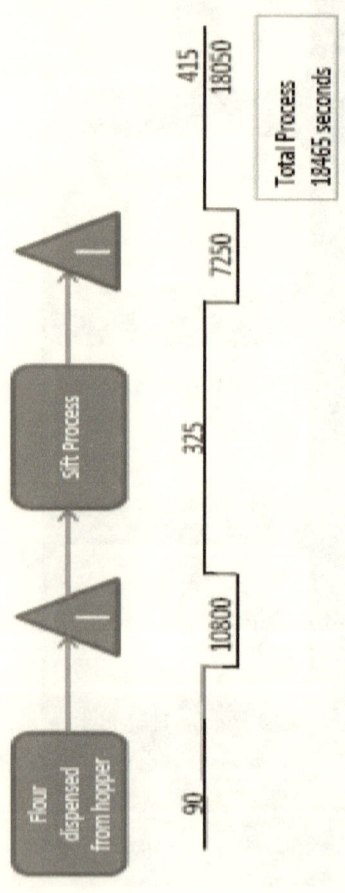

(Diagram 4.4)

If we analyse the VSM, of the total 18,465 seconds for the process only 415 are value adding or incidental. The balance of 18,050 seconds is pure waste in the value stream. That equates to 97% of the lead time for this process being non value adding.

So a push system will generally result in a build up of inventory between processes. This inventory can lead to many issues:

- Poor Quality
- Increased Safety Risks
- Increased Scrap
- Poor Cashflow

The way to control these issues is to introduce a pull system. A pull system usually uses some form of kanban to control the "pull" of the product through the manufacturing process. The word kanban is Japanese and means a trigger – usually a card.

To simply explain; a kanban is used to trigger something else to occur. Diagram 4.5 briefly shows how a kanban system works.

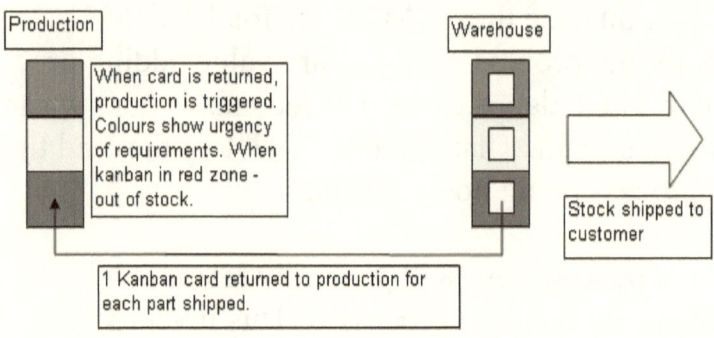

(Diagram 4.5)

In this instance, we are using kanban cards and two corresponding kanban boards. When the warehouse ship a part the kanban card for that part is sent to the production kanban board as a trigger to produce another part.

There are two main types of kanban systems:

- Withdrawal kanban
- Production kanban

Withdrawal kanban systems utilise a supermarket of stock which is drawn upon. When stock is withdrawn a kanban triggers the part to be replenished. This system allows for reduced and planned inventory to be maintained, however because inventory still exists may not be suitable where a great variety of parts are produced. Often in these circumstances a supermarket of high volume parts is maintained in conjunction with other systems for the lower volume products.

Production kanban systems operate in a similar fashion, however do not hold inventory. So when a part is required, a kanban is sent to the previous process or supplier to manufacture or deliver the product. These systems allow for far reduced inventory, however they do require on time delivery from all suppliers (both internal and external). It is a good practice to set up and use a withdrawal kanban system for any high volume products and utilise production kanban systems for lower volume or less critical products unless your systems to control the suppliers and supplier processes are robust enough to ensure on time delivery.

CAPACITY PLANNING MODEL

Capacity planning is another tool that can be implemented to ensure JIT is successful. To introduce capacity planning you first need to know the capacity of your processes. This may seem to be stating the obvious, but it is surprising how often businesses try to implement this without knowing!

The only way to know the capacity of your machines and processes is to measure their relative outputs. What do I mean by relative outputs? This simply means to measure the outputs that are controlled by the cycle. An example of this would be a brake press machine – I often see managers measuring the output of completed parts from the process even though some parts have multiple bends. The only relevant measure of this process is the number of cycles completed per shift (unless you are interested in product mix). The actual number of cycles when compared to the available capacity will assist in identifying lost capacity.

Most MRP and ERP systems enable capacity planning of some type. If you are not utilising one of these systems, a simple spreadsheet can be developed to assist with capacity planning.

HOW IS AN "IDEAL STATE" DEVELOPED?

The most important thing to understand is that this ideal state must be free from as many obstacles as possible. Remember anything is possible – if it seems impossible then you just haven't worked out how it can be done. Look around you now and look at the technology that would have seemed impossible only 10 years ago!

Free thinking is a skill that can be learned and just like most other skills, the more practice you get the better you will become. Free thinking as an individual can be a difficult thing to master, however group free thinking whilst being more difficult is extremely powerful when facilitated effectively.

One of the best tools that can be used to facilitate group free thinking is undoubtedly brainstorming. Brainstorming is simply a session where every person is encouraged to suggest ideas to fix a problem, it is important to make it very clear that every idea is a good idea and that all suggestions are recorded on the white board without prejudice.

Often the best ideas will come from what are first thought to be far fetched suggestions. As the initial idea is built upon by the group, these seeds can grow into great ideas. Brainstorming can be conducted formally and informally.

When conducted formally the process is structured as a mind mapping or cause and effect session.

- Each participant takes a turn to add a suggestion
- The benefits of this structured approach is that all participants add value
- The facilitator needs to be confident and experienced to get the best outcome.

When conducted informally the there is limited structure to the process.

- Participants are encouraged to add suggestions freely
- The benefit of this approach is the team can quickly come up with a large number of ideas
- Another problem is that one or more participants can hijack the activity – an experienced facilitator can limit the effects and likelihood of this

During this process it is important that the facilitator keeps the participants on track and that the team does not debate the suitability of any ideas or that intimidation does not occur.

Mind mapping is a form of brainstorming when the ideas are written on the board, as more ideas are added the facilitator begins to group the similar ideas together. Ideas that are built on others are shown in a parent / sibling relationship. Mind mapping is best used when the team is working well together and the ideas are flowing freely. It is not a good idea to try and force this structure onto a team that is not functioning effectively as the result will likely be ineffective.

It is important to work through the value stream when brainstorming for countermeasures and not try to find countermeasures for every problem area at the same time. This may take many sessions before the ideal state is finalised. Fix one problem area first then go onto the next. It is a good idea to have an area of the board boxed off to write down any ideas that come up that may be useful for problems other that the focus.

I am always surprised to see teams getting bogged down during the development of their ideal state. This is the step that I get the most from as I can challenge myself to find new innovative ways to overcome issues and I also get great personal satisfaction in seeing a team that I am involved with doing the same.

After identifying the countermeasures there are a couple of ways to determine which one to use (assuming that more than one countermeasure has been identified).

1. Consensus
   This can be useful for teams that know each other and have been working together for some time. Be mindful of group think (see insert next page).
2. Multi-voting
   This is a useful tool that has a number of guises. Basically each participant is given a set number of votes to allocate the selection of countermeasures. This allocation can be anonymous or open. Once all votes have been allocated, the votes are counted and the selection with the greatest number of votes is the chosen option.

Group Think

Group think is a term that was phrased by psychologist Irving Janis in 1972. This is a situation that occurs when a group working together gain a false consensus.

To make groupthink testable, Irving Janis devised eight symptoms indicative of groupthink (1977).

1. *Illusions of invulnerability* creating excessive optimism and encouraging risk taking.
2. *Rationalising warnings* that might challenge the group's assumptions.
3. *Unquestioned belief* in the morality of the group, causing members to ignore the consequences of their actions.
4. *Stereotyping* those who are opposed to the group as weak, evil, biased, spiteful, disfigured, impotent, or stupid.
5. *Direct pressure* to conform placed on any member who questions the group, couched in terms of "disloyalty".
6. *Self censorship* of ideas that deviate from the apparent group consensus.
7. *Illusions of unanimity* among group members, silence is viewed as agreement.
8. *Mindguards* — self-appointed members who shield the group from dissenting information.

Another take on multi-voting is the Nominal Group Technique. This is similar to multi-voting however the options are entered into a grid and identified as A, B, C etc. The participants then rank the options from 1 to X (being the number of options). After all participants have ranked the options, the scores are tallied similarly to multi-voting.

This process will continue until all of the problem areas have countermeasures allocated against them. It is a good idea to regularly review the status of the project against the project scope as it is very easy to veer away from the original scope. A good way to ensure the potential for this to occur is reduced is to use what is termed a "parking lot" – this is a separate list of open issues and new opportunities that are outside of the scope of the current project.

After determining all of the required countermeasures a new value stream map, material flow diagram, process map are developed. Examples of these tools can be seen in the appendices.

TIME TO GET REALISTIC…

Remember that all of the above has been developed to be an ideal state. In most situations we cannot implement this ideal state as there are likely to be resource issues that make some changes impractical. These issues may be financial, time, labour among others.

To implement the improvements we need to be realistic about what we can implement now. The reason we begin by designing an ideal state is that is easier to bring an ideal state back to reality than to stretch a reality further. Now it is time to look at each of the improvements or countermeasures and assess them.

PFMEA

Failure Modes and Effects Analysis were first developed by the US military in the 1940's to determine any potential failures in plans. It didn't take long for the same tools to be used in businesses. Now FMEA's are an important and common place tool used when developing new products and processes.

There are two common types of FMEA's:

DFMEA (Design Failure Modes and Effects Analysis) are used in the early stages of designing a new product or when significant changes are made to an existing product.

PFMEA (Process Failure Modes and Effects Analysis) are used when designing a new process to be introduced or when significant changes are made to an existing process.

When performing a PFMEA, the potential risks are ranked against certain criteria for their severity, occurrence (likelihood) and detection (likelihood). These rankings are scored from 1 through to 10.

For severity, a score of 1 can be described as having no discernable effect, whereas a score of 10 is likely to have strong safety and or government regulatory implications.

For occurrence, a score of 1 can be attributed to a very low or remote potential for occurrence, whereas a score of 10 indicates a very high potential for occurrence.

For detection, a score of 1 will indicate that the detection is almost certain through engineering means, whereas a score of 10 indicates a near total lack of detection means (in this instance it is likely that any defects will NOT be detected).

These rankings or scores are then multiplied to output an RPN (Risk Priority Number). This number is used to determine the controls and countermeasures that will be needed to ensure the process is robust.

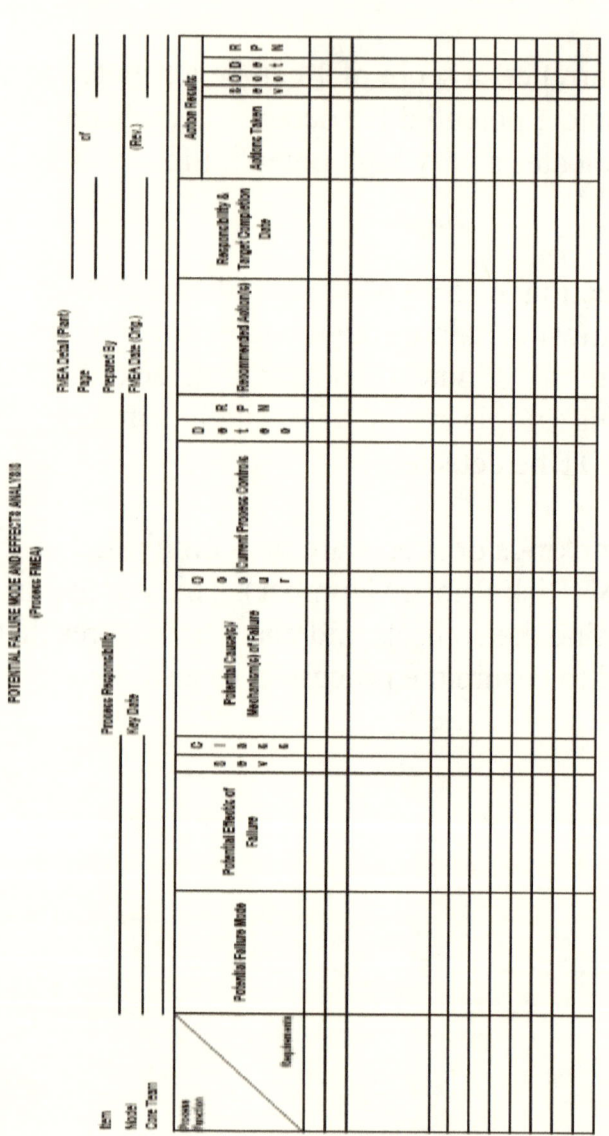

(Diagram 4.6)

A PFMEA can be a valuable tool when designing any new or revised process. By understanding, controlling or eliminating potential risks or failures before implantation you will ensure success.

Chapter 5

What is the difference?

To assess each of the countermeasures we first perform a gap analysis of the current state to the future or ideal state. A gap analysis is a simple tool used to define the difference between two situations.

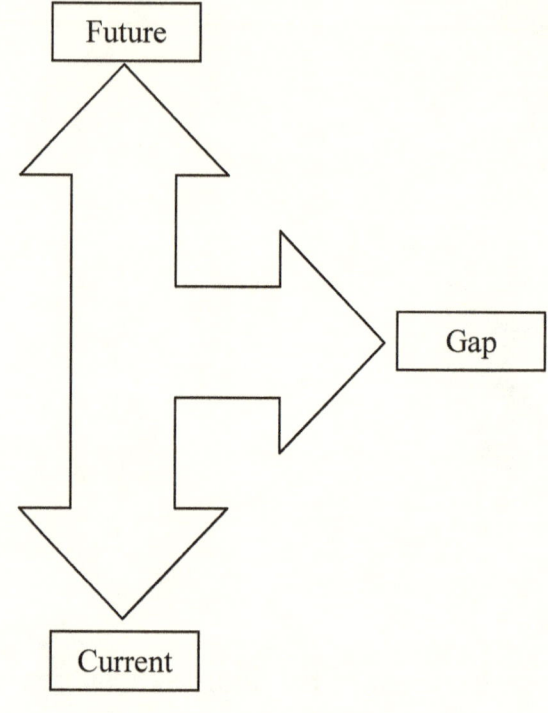

(Diagram 5.1)

The above diagram (5.1) shows the classic gap analysis. This can be used to identify gaps in KPI's or as in this instance gaps in processes. Below is an example of how a gap analysis can be used to identify the difference between a current and ideal state (Diagram 5.2).

The gap analysis can be used to define the different options available to achieve the desired outcome as in diagram 5.2 or to show the chosen option for a presentation. Either way it is a powerful tool.

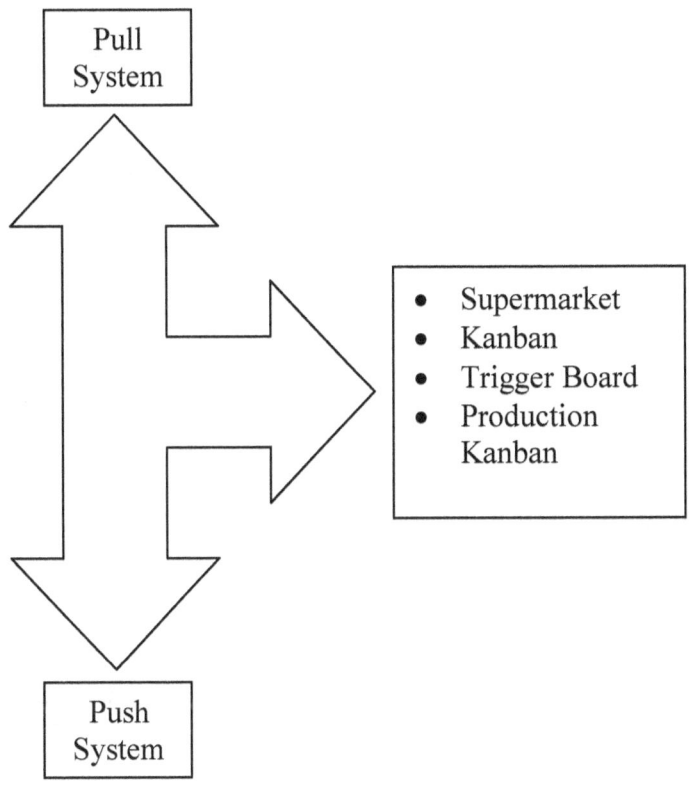

(Diagram 5.2)

In the above example, we have the current state being a push system and the desired outcome being a pull system. The gap analysis shows the options available to enable the pull system to be introduced. Used in this way, the gap analysis is a simple tool to clearly define the options to move forward. It is important to define these options to enable the team to choose effectively.

The gaps need to be analysed in this way for each countermeasure or option put forward to achieve the future state. Before this is undertaken, it is necessary to weed out any truly inappropriate choices. Otherwise this task will become too big and cumbersome. Even when the process being changed is a relatively small one, there will be many options for the future state and each of these will have any number of options to achieve it.

The outcome from this will be a list of future state ideas and a corresponding list of options to make getting there possible. The list of options is where we will now work to design exactly how the future will look.

As usual there are a number of tools that can be used to determine the most suitable future state. We will look at some of these tools now.

FORCE FIELD ANALYSIS

A force field analysis is a useful tool that can be used to determine the benefits and drawbacks of a proposal. The benefits and drawbacks of the proposal are compared side by side on a single sheet to enable the users to gain a clear understanding of the potential of the proposed concept.

The best time to use a force field analysis is when there are two contradicting alternatives as in this situation the benefits of one option may well be the drawbacks of the other. This tool can be used effectively when comparing two similar alternatives. A force field analysis should be undertaken by a team rather than in isolation, this is the case for most if the tools used. Diagram 5.3 shows an example of a blank force field analysis work sheet.

(Diagram 5.3)

To begin the analysis, the top section of the worksheet is filled in with the date and the names of the team.

Now, a concise description of the change proposal is entered into the centre block. The team then discusses all of the forces FOR the change and enters these in the left column. Next the team discussed all of the forces AGAINST the change.

The next step is to assign a score for each force for and against. A score of 1 indicates a weak force; a score of 5 indicates a strong force. This can be performed by utilising multi voting or a similar system. The scores are then added and entered into the totals blocks. Diagram 5.4 is a completed example of a force field analysis.

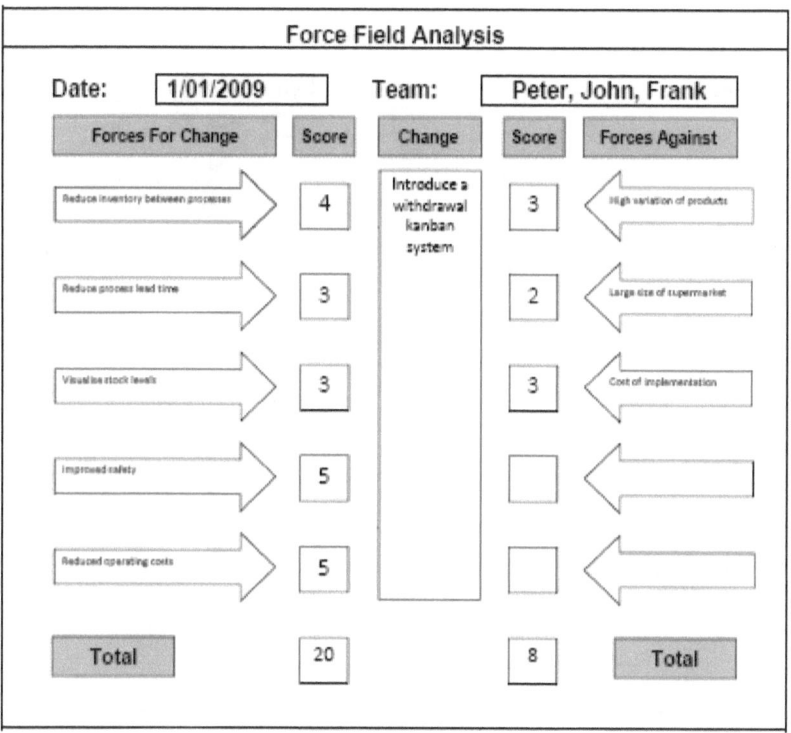

(Diagram 5.4)

In this example it is an obvious choice to go with a withdrawal kanban system. It is a good idea however to use this tool to compare this option with another alternative. Now we will look at a force field analysis for a trigger kanban system in diagram 5.5 to show the benefits of a comparison.

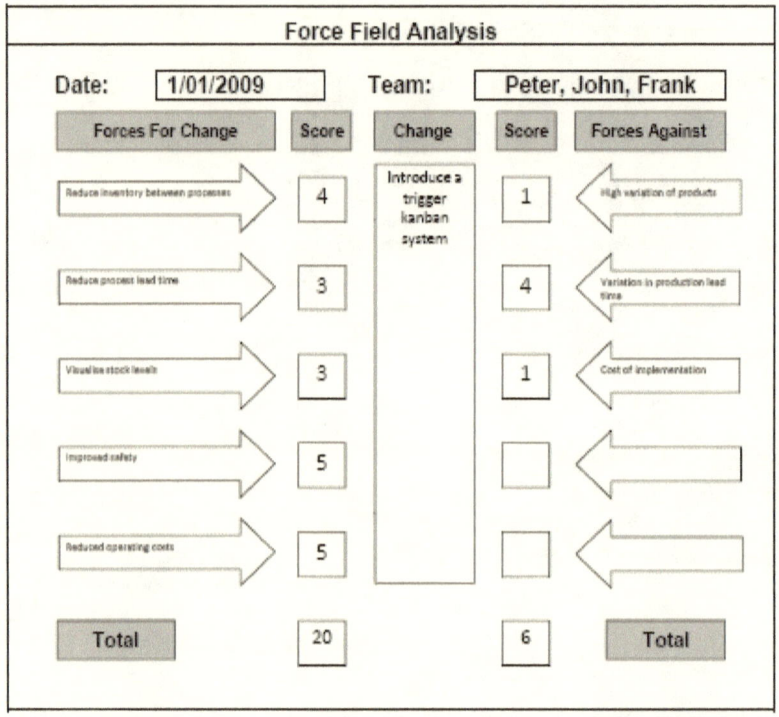

(Diagram 5.5)

As we can see in this example a trigger kanban system may in fact be a more suitable solution than a withdrawal system due to the high variety of products and the size of supermarket required to support it. This example has the same FOR score as the previous example but has a lower against score. This leads us to the outcome of introducing a trigger kanban system.

A force field analysis can be performed in a situation where there are more than two options, however this will obviously become more cumbersome as the number of options increases. The force field analysis enables the team to follow a logical decision making process to identify the most suitable option.

COUNTERMEASURE ANALYSIS MATRIX

A countermeasure analysis matrix (CA Matrix) is a tool is derived from a matrix often used in marketing assessments called the positioning or perceptual map.

The matrix is divided into 4 quadrants:

- High Cost - Low Impact
- High Cost - High Impact
- Low Cost - Low Impact
- Low Cost - High Impact

The options are listed and numbered; for example Option 1 through to Option 8. This list is used as a legend for the CA Matrix. After this the options are entered into the matrix.

Where to position the options on the matrix is determined by the two criteria of cost and impact. At this point in time this is based on estimated cost and potential impact (although the potential impact will not be known before implementation, it can be closely estimated). Diagram 5.6 is an example of a CA Matrix with no data added.

(Diagram 5.6)

In diagram 5.7 the example has been completed with the options 1 through 9 added.

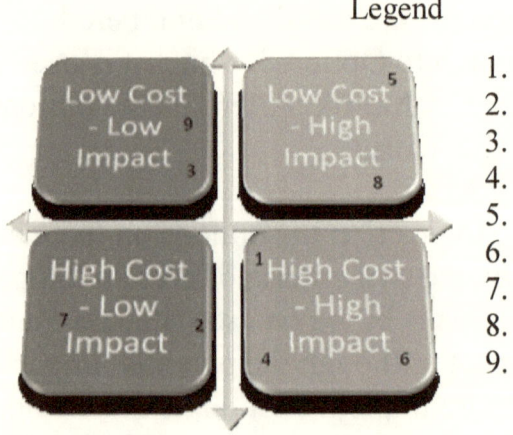

Legend

1.
2.
3.
4.
5.
6.
7.
8.
9.

(Diagram 5.7)

The higher the cost the more towards the bottom of the matrix the option is positioned. The higher the potential impact the further towards the right the option is positioned. By following this positioning formula it is clear that in the example above, option 5 is the better option as it provides the highest potential impact with the lowest cost.

The axis can be renamed to give different criteria. For example, when training 5S I will usually use Time and Cost as the two criteria to identify the improvements that are quick to implement.

The CA Matrix can be used in any situation where you have multiple options, however it is best used with between five and nine alternatives.

COWS ANALYSIS

The COWS analysis is a useful tool that can be used to analyse almost any situation. COWS stands for:

- Challenges: looks at the internal and external factors that may have a negative impact to a successful implementation

- Opportunities: looks at the internal and external factors that may assist in the successful implementation

- Weaknesses: looks at how this change may negatively impact on the business or any business component

- Strengths: looks at how this change will positively impact the business or business component

Unlike the SWOT (strengths, weaknesses, opportunities and threats) analysis, the COWS analysis looks at supporting factors e.g. relationships; before looking at the tangible factors. This provides a more thorough understanding of the current situation and ensures the supporting factors are analysed.

It is often underestimated (until hindsight kicks in) how critical the support of internal and external factors can be on a project. We often discuss, at great length, the project with those that are seen to be directly involved. We need to communicate with the departments and people that may not be directly involved but may be directly or indirectly impacted. This impact could be positive or negative; it doesn't really matter. The fact that communication did not occur will have a negative impact on the project.

The COWS analysis helps us to identify who we need to communicate to as it defines what challenges we are likely to face along the way and also who can be our allies. This is another tool that has been developed from a marketing tool. In many ways managing change in an organisation is similar to marketing a product or service. We need to identify what the customer (the business) needs and firstly "sell" the plan to different parts of the business.

A COWS analysis is simply a matrix of four quadrants. These quadrants are labelled Challenges, Opportunities, Weaknesses and Strengths. Diagram 5.8 shows an example of a typical COWS analysis.

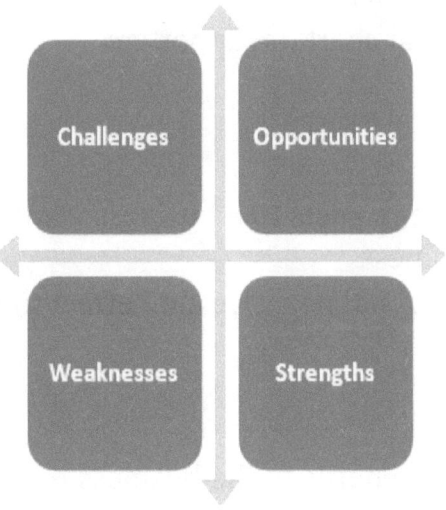

(Diagram 5.8)

As every project is invariably different it is difficult to provide examples of the four criteria however below is a brief list.

Challenges:

- Interaction with internal / external suppliers
- Interactions with internal / external customers
- Management commitment and support

Opportunities:

- Probable support from internal / external suppliers and customers
- Hierarchal chart of supporters

Weaknesses

- Negative impacts to a business component or to the business
- Unintentional negative side effect to the process

Strengths

- Positive benefits to the business or business component
- Further improvement opportunities available due to the impacts of this project

The COWS analysis is usually used to further analyse an opportunity prior to testing, yet after some of the previous tools have been used.

Up until this point in time we have been working in the Plan stage of the PDCA cycle. Now it is time to begin looking at Do. Do basically means to test some of the theories that have become the Plan.

It is in this stage of the cycle that you will run pilot programs, simulations etc. It is important that these be structured effectively.

THINK LIKE A SCIENTIST

Now, you don't have to go around in a white lab coat if you don't want to but if it helps....

By thinking like a scientist it is referring to a logical, data driven and methodical approach to the trials.

Remember back in school, when you performed experiments in Science. You would ask a question, make a statement as an expected outcome and then test your hypothesis. It is the same with the trials being conducted in this stage.

The question is the gap identified earlier and the answer or statement would be the countermeasures put forward. The trails conducted are testing your hypothesis.

A trial worksheet can be used to record and measure the effectiveness of a trial. The outcome will either be effective or ineffective, the only situation where a trial will be unsuccessful is when the data is not clear or the trial cannot be completed for any reason.

The basic steps to conducting a trial are outline below.

1) Plan the trial
   a. Define the scope
   b. Determine the team
   c. Conduct training
   d. State the expected outcome
2) Conduct the trial

3) Record outcomes
    a. Record data
    b. Safety issues
    c. Processing issues
    d. Documentation issues
    e. Any other issues
4) Check

Now we are entering the check phase of the PDCA cycle. This is where we are going to compare the outcomes from our trials and simulations against our expected outcomes.

WHY IS THIS SO IMPORTANT?

I mentioned at the start of this book that continuous improvement is not something new, but is a hard wired human trait; without it we would not have progressed past the original stone tools used. How does this relate to checking? Well, it took thousands of years to move on from stone tools, yet decades to move from slide rules to the computers we have today. This is due to a change in scientific concepts during the middle ages when we began analysing our outcomes and comparing these to the expectations.

This shows the importance of checking results of trials against the expected outcomes. It is at the checking stage that a decision has to be made.

Did the trial prove the new process to be capable? There are three clear answers to this question.

A) No – If the trial did not prove the process to capable then you will need to move back to the Plan stage. Make the necessary changes and run another trial.
B) Yes – If the trial clearly proves that the new process is capable without doubt then the plans can be made permanent as you move onto that "Act" stage. This will be discussed in a later chapter.
C) Yes, "but" – The dreaded but! Unfortunately this is the same as a "No" you have to go back to the plan stage (however briefly) and make the necessary changes to the plan.

Chapter 6

How Do We Get There?

You may have thought we would finally be moving into the Act stage, not yet! Before we start acting we need to plan again. This is the action plan and is a detailed plan of the actions that need to be taken to achieve the end goals.

Where this step fits into the overall plan can be argued. Many will say this should to be set before we go onto Do and Act, however I am yet to be involved in a project where this has actually occurred effectively.

The reason for this is the changes and amendments that are made after the trails and experiments are run in the DO stage. If we had taken the time to make the action plan or the detailed activity plan as it is often referred to before the trials then we would have to review and modify the plan. These modifications are often so great that it in my opinion that to wait until after the trials to make the action plan. I actually have a step in the initial activity plan to compile the action plan.

PROJECT MANAGEMENT

The role of the project leader can be very similar to that of a project manager. After the project is identified and chosen, then the role of the project leader is to facilitate the successful implementation of the project.

If your role is to facilitate the project then it is important to remember your role. It is very easy to become too involved in the actual implementation of changes. If it is agreed that this is your role then it is fine to get involved, however the role of a project leader is big enough as a facilitator alone without the added workload of implementing.

ACTION PLAN / DETAILED ACTIVITY PLAN

As discussed above, the action plan is the step by step actions that must be completed to successfully complete the project. A blank copy of an action plan is in Appendix 4.

As the scope of the project increases, the importance of the action plan also increases. It is absolutely crucial that the action plan is complete, concise (so it is easy to read and follow), and just like any other targets or goals (each of the actions should be looked at as individual goals) the actions need to be SMART.

SMART

I'm sure you have heard of SMART goals before now.

Specific – Be as specific as possible
Measurable – You have to be in a position to know when the goal is achieved
Attainable – Is the action within the control of the person responsible
Relevant - Will the completion of the action provide to required results
Time – Give each action a time frame for completion

A mnemonic that you may not have heard is STAR goals and targets.

Specific - As above
Target– Give each goal a target
Actions – As attainable above
Responsible – Assign responsibility for every action to a person (not a department)
I like to use the STAR goal setting method in conjunction with the SMART method. Smart is used when setting goals and STAR is used when measuring or displaying goals or targets.

A small sample of an action plan is below. As you can see, this follows the STAR principle with a cell for the Status, a Target or due date and Responsibility is assigned.

This action plan should be completed as a team with all responsible people present. Only those people present should be assigned responsibility, this doesn't mean they cannot delegate the action to another employee, however in the meeting a person (not a department) needs to accept responsibility for the completion of the task.

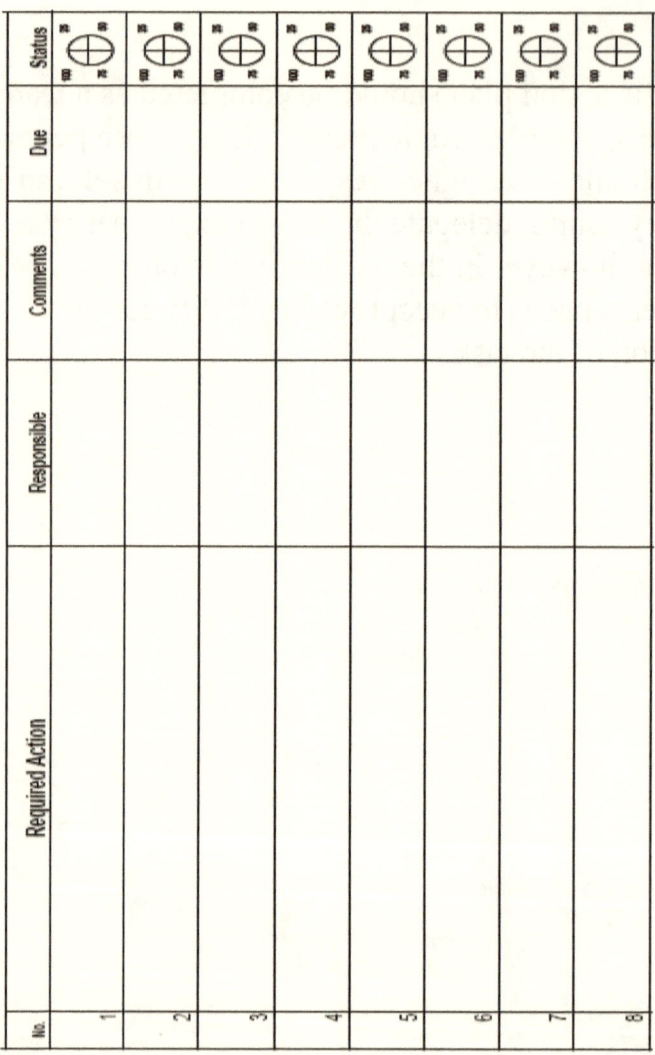

(Figure 6.1)

PROJECT TRACKING / STATUS

As a leader of a project it is important to stay on top of the action status and the project adherence to schedule. When something is overdue it is too late to find out why; you need to know soon enough to be able to put into place some corrective measures.

How you go about tracking the progress and status will largely be determined by a number of factors including:

- The importance or critical nature of the project
- The project timing
- The physical location of the project to your location
- The size of the working team and their locations

The methods of tracking the status of the project can include:

- Planned meeting schedule
- Informal updates
  - Face to face
  - Emails
  - Telephone
- Planned update schedule
  - Emails
  - Reports

As a project leader it is necessary to update other stakeholders (these can be internal or external). Whether necessary or not, it is a good practice to follow as long as you do not fall into the trap of over communicating. An easy way to communicate the status and progress of the project is to display the activity plan, action plan or Gantt chart on display boards in relevant areas. Alternatively you can be more formal and update with a report. Either way the practice of updating stakeholders assists your role by eliminating the flow of requests for information that you will likely receive as a project leader.

Another advantage of effective communication is consensus. Awareness of the action plan by all stakeholders eliminates any surprises and the impacts they can create.

Often, just when changes are about to be implemented a lone challenge can rise from nowhere and stall the activity. Regardless of consensus meetings, there is often someone who didn't know of the changes. By displaying the action plan in a conspicuous location this problem can be reduced.

PLANNING TOOLS

There are many planning tools that can be used to make the management of a project easier. Although not absolutely necessary (people managed for many generations without many of these tools), they will ensure the journey is trouble free when used correctly.

GANTT CHART

A Gantt chart is basically a bar graph that is used to illustrate a project schedule. This tool was developed by Henry Gantt in the early 20th century.

Advantages:
- Shows starts and planned finish times of project actions
- Can show dependencies between activities
- Critical path
- Milestones can be added
- Universal use
- Large availability of software

Limitations / Disadvantages
- Large projects can become difficult to follow
- Can become difficult to view on screen or print
- Difficult to manage larger projects

PERT CHART

A PERT chart is more like a flow chart with the steps involved in the project replacing the processes. PERT stands for "Program Evaluation and Review Technique" and has been developed over many years. This method was refined by Henry Ford.

It is often used in conjunction with other tools as a decision making tool.

Advantages:
- Easy to follow the critical path of the project
- Contains information on early start, late start, early finish and late finish for each activity
- Can enable reduce project lead time due to increased visibility of dependencies and critical path

Limitations / Disadvantages
- Potential for very large number of dependency relationships
- Status of project and individual activities can be unclear, particularly with single colour printing
- Physical size of plan can become excessive, requiring special paper sizes

SAMPLE PERT CHART

TIMELINE

As the name suggests this is a timeline for the project with milestones set and tracked. The length of the time line can vary depending on the size and planned period of the project.

Advantages:
- Easy to understand
- Logical layout
- Can be tracked and monitored against original version

Limitations / Disadvantages
- The length of the timeline can become excessive for longer projects
- Can become messy with complicated projects or projects with many milestones

CALENDAR

For many smaller projects or projects that continue over a very long period of time, a calendar may be an effective tool to plan the project.

Advantages:
- Readily available
- Reminders can be set
- Tasks can be assigned to project members
- Work completed can be tracked and reports derived

Limitations / Disadvantages
- Printing of project plan difficult
- High level of discipline required to maintain project

The best method to use will depend on the project and team involved. I usually use a combination of these tools to manage projects. Depending on the size and nature of the project I use Gantt or PERT charts to plan out the project and my standard PC calendar software to manage the tasks, set reminders and assign tasks to other team members.

SOFTWARE

For all of the planning tools, there is now software available to make the job easier to manage. Whichever software you use or even if you manage your projects manually, it takes discipline to manage any project effectively.

The more milestones included in the project, the more important this discipline is. To plan a project and expect tasks to be completed without management is naïve. Regular monitoring, updating and communication is essential for a successful project.

Chapter 7

Implementation

Finally we have made it! We can now implement the changes and see the improvements taking place in our business. There are a few techniques that can be used to ensure the changes are more effective. These techniques will be discussed in the following pages. Some of the techniques work well in combinations.

LEADERS IN ACTION

By involving the business, department and project leaders in the implementation of the changes it is more likely that the improvements will be taken seriously. Involvement by the leaders shows that the changes are important to the business.

Another good reason to involve the leaders in the implementation is to ensure the leaders and managers understand how the changes work and the impact they have on the business and workforce. Often, when the leaders are not involved, the impacts of the changes are not understood. This can lead to assumptions by the leaders based on ignorance.

Team morale will be improved with the involvement of the leadership group. This is because with their involvement the respect of the entire workforce will be improved. With increased morale you will realise improved communication between management and the workforce.

Get your management involved in the implementation.

IMPLEMENTATION WITH THE WORKFORCE

By involving the work force in any implementation of change you will create ownership of the new process. This ownership will enable the new process to become to the standard or "this is how we've always done it."

Achieving this new standard is critical in sustainability, without it when times are busy or understaffed, the process is likely to revert back. Often as soon you turn your attention to the next project, the process reverts back. This will lead to reduced morale and difficulty with future projects.

Apart from ownership, this involvement from the workforce will instil a sense of pride in the department. Don't underestimate the power of pride in work, although most people will not admit it this can be a very powerful motivator.

BE PREPARED

When implementing any new process into an existing operation it is likely that there will be some degree of chaos during the transition period. Just how much chaos and how this impacts on the business can be controlled by preparation.

In chapter 4 we introduced the PFMEA, a tool used to determine the potential failures of the new process and define how these will be controlled. This tool can also be used in preparation for implementation to control how the transition period will impact the business.

All stakeholders need to be involved in this vital step; initially this may be difficult to get involvement but you will later find the same stakeholders who are hesitant to be involved will make the loudest noise when the chaos starts.

List all of the potential issues in a brainstorming session, everything the team can come up with is written down. Have the team rank these in priority of severity, occurrence and detection to determine the RPN. Then, beginning with the highest RPN, determine the countermeasures and controls for the failures. Put in place as many of the controls as possible before any implementation of the changes begins.

By following this you will encounter less issues and it is possible to keep peoples emotions under control.

WHAT TO EXPECT?

When faced with change people commonly have reservations. To say people are scared of change is probably inaccurate, however many people are scared of the unknown future that change may trigger. There is a subtle yet significant difference between being scared of change and scared of the unknown, because if these differences it is necessary to approach the two differently.

Almost every person I have encountered in my time facilitating change in organisations has shown a fear of the unknown to some degree. Until I recognised this as a fear of the unknown and not a fear of change I found it hard for people to acknowledge their fears.

I would say to them "it is normal to fear change but it's important in your position to push through that fear and make a difference." On and on I could go and the other person would hear less and less because as they were telling me they weren't really afraid of change but the unknown.

Now I say "it is normal for people to fear the unknown", and they agree. We can then move on to discuss how they can best overcome this fear. Like most fear, often the best medicine is to slowly be touched by the fear.

Some people enjoy change and the associated unknown future. If you can find a person with this mindset, make them a big part of the team. Their enthusiasm for change will rub off onto the rest of the team and go along way to dealing with any fear issues. For a project manager, dealing with fears can become a full time activity – you may feel like a counsellor at times – however, when managed early these same team members can become your most valuable assets as they overcome their own fears, they will drag other along with them.

CELEBRATE YOUR EFFORTS

It is important to hold some sort of celebration upon the completion or handover of a project. What this celebration is will depend on many different criteria:

- Business Type
- Business Culture

- Project Size
- Team Size / Relationships

Whatever celebrations you choose make sure to include all stake holders and team members. It is important to celebrate as soon as possible after the completion of the project.

AUDIT

As part of every project you should include an audit of the implemented process before & after handover.

The pre-handover audit is to ensure the process is working as planned and all accountabilities are clearly understood.

A post handover audit should be held at 1 month and 3 month s after handing over to determine the effectiveness of the process and also to ensure the required discipline.

These audits should be undertaken by the project leader, owner and sponsor. These people need to be involved in the audit as they understand the process and also have the authority to make decisions.

HANDOVER

The handing over of a project is one of the most important steps in any improvement activity.

A simple handover checklist is shown below.

Continuous Improvement Project Handover Form			
Project Title			
Project Team			
Handover Date			
Item	Required?	Comp. (Y / N) ?	Comment
Registered Procedure			
Registered Work Instructions			
Risk Assesment	Y		
Training Forms			
CI Process Validation Form			
KPI's set, understood and documented (below)			
BOM's Updated			
KPI #	Name		Target
KPI # 1			
Title	Name		Signature / Date

Another good idea is to validate the process before handing over. This should be undertaken over 1 month.

The idea is to test the new process while actually in use. This form is filled out at the end of the month, signed off by the stakeholders and then forms part of the handover package.

The handover package should include:

- Process Validation Form
- Project Handover Form
- Risk Assessment
- Documented Processes
- Work Instructions
- Training Documentation
- KPI's
  - o KPI recording / analysis documents

Continuous Improvement Process Validation Form		
Project Title		
Project Team		
Introduction Date		

Item	Comment	Closed (Y/N)
Are there any safety concerns / issues?		
Are there any environmental concerns / issues		
Are all required tools available to complete the process / tasks		
Are all processes / instructions clear?		
Are responsibilities clearly defined?		
Is the process resourced effectively?		
Are there any specific areas of improvement?		

Title	Name	Signature / Date

SUSTAIN

You can only be certain that you have successfully implemented the new process when it is sustained. In other words the new process become the "This is how we always do it".

Sustainability can be difficult to attain. Some helpful ideas to give you the best opportunity to achieve sustainability are listed below:

- Management support and drive
- Complete stakeholder buy-in
- Set relevant KPI's
- Open communication
- Strategic deployment of improvement resources
- Structured reporting system (KPI's)
- Departmental goals / targets aligned with corporate strategies

Chapter 8
Where To Now?

You should already have the answer to this question. Any improvement activity should be a part of a lean business strategy. Below is diagram of the lean business process.

This diagram shows the relationship between the corporate vision, strategy and goals and how these form the Lean Business Strategy. It is similar to a funnel with the vision being a broad concept of what the company wants to achieve. This is transformed into the business strategy. Goals are set to enable the strategy to succeed. These goals are analysed for gaps to identify the lean strategies.

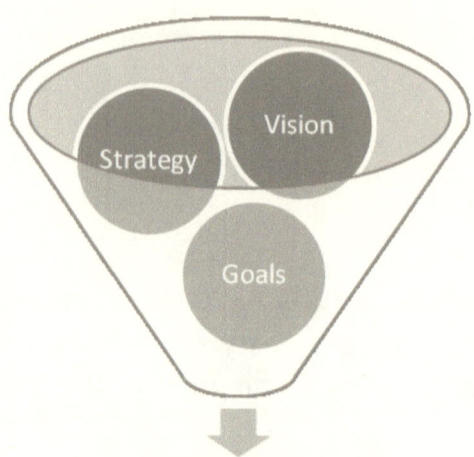

Lean Business Strategy

Another way to show this relationship is shown in the simple process diagram below.

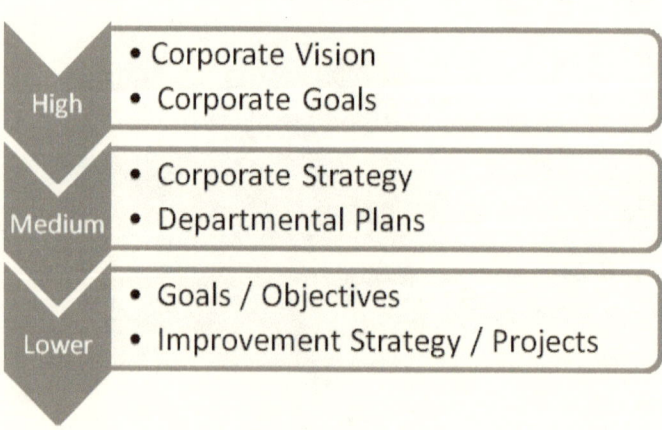

The development of a lean business strategy can take some time, however this time will be quickly repaid by ensuring you have a sustainable improvement program.

Appendix 1

Get the most from your photographs

They say a picture paints a thousand words. This is so very true - if it's the right picture. There is nothing better than displaying a great picture in a presentation and hearing the audience collectively gasp.

Although it seems easy to take a photo, getting the right photo for the situation is a skill that should be practiced. Getting the right photo is a combination of a few skills:

- Photography
  - o Technical ability
- Decision
  - o Which photo to choose
- Application
  - o How to format the photo
- Discipline
  - o Use these skills consistently

There are some simple steps that can be followed to give your photos the greatest impact.

- Take as many photos as practical
- Save only those worthwhile for the application

- Choose the perspective carefully
- Take future photos from the same position / perspective
- Work with the natural light – careful of reflections, refracting light and shadows
- A good photo needs no explanation
- Position for a clean background
- Choose the elevation of the shot

Good photography skills and presentation skills will help you in winning support for a project

Appendix 2
Examples

Current State VSM

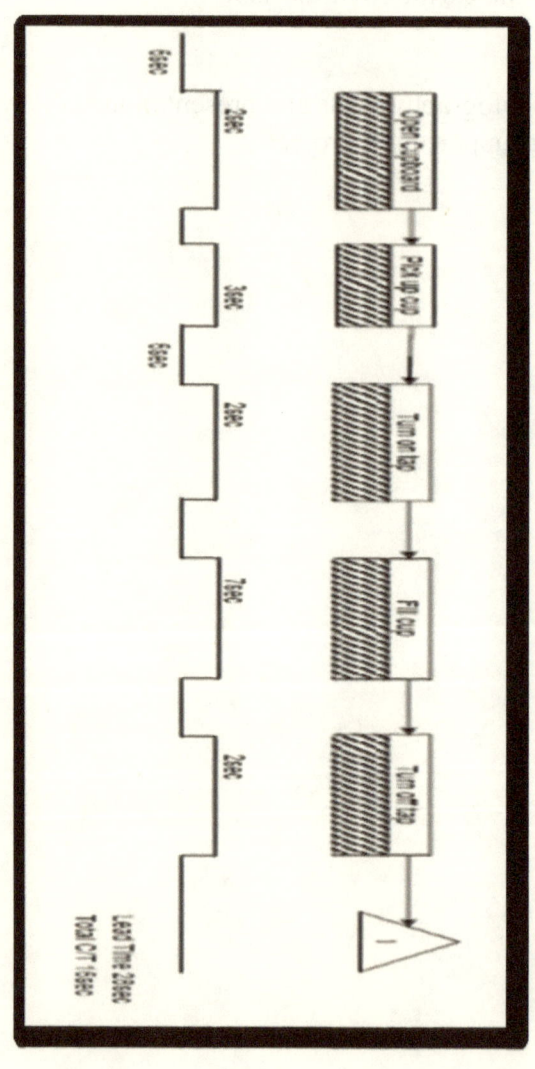

Future State VSM

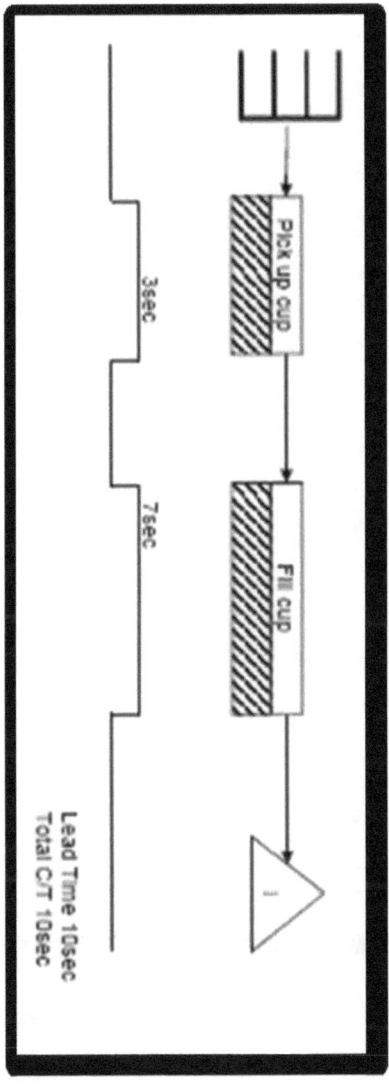

Process Map

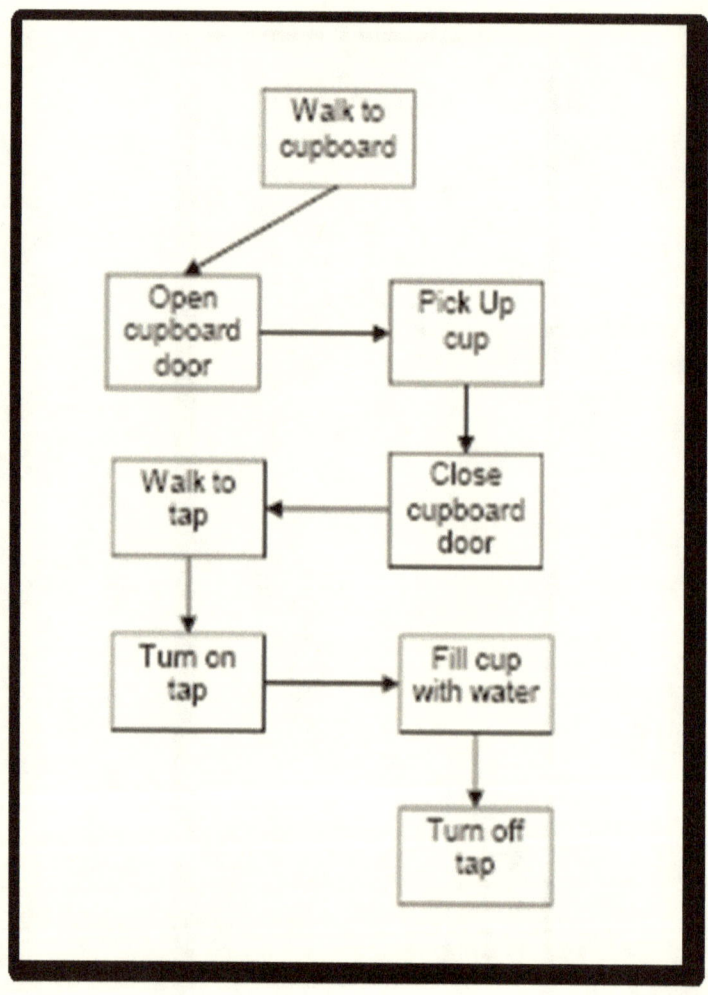

Process Study

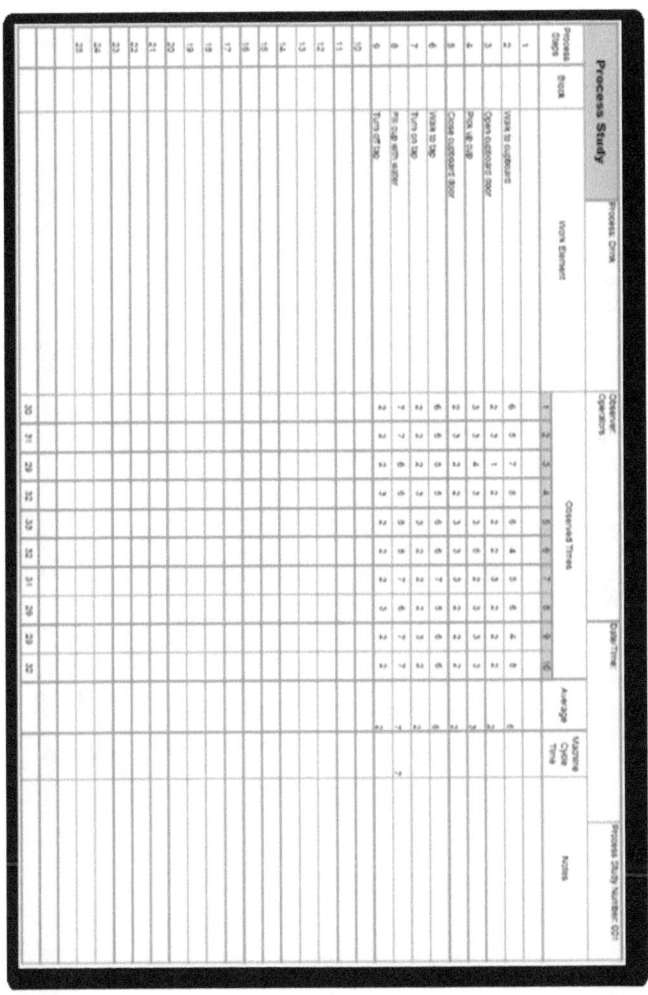

Material Flow Diagram

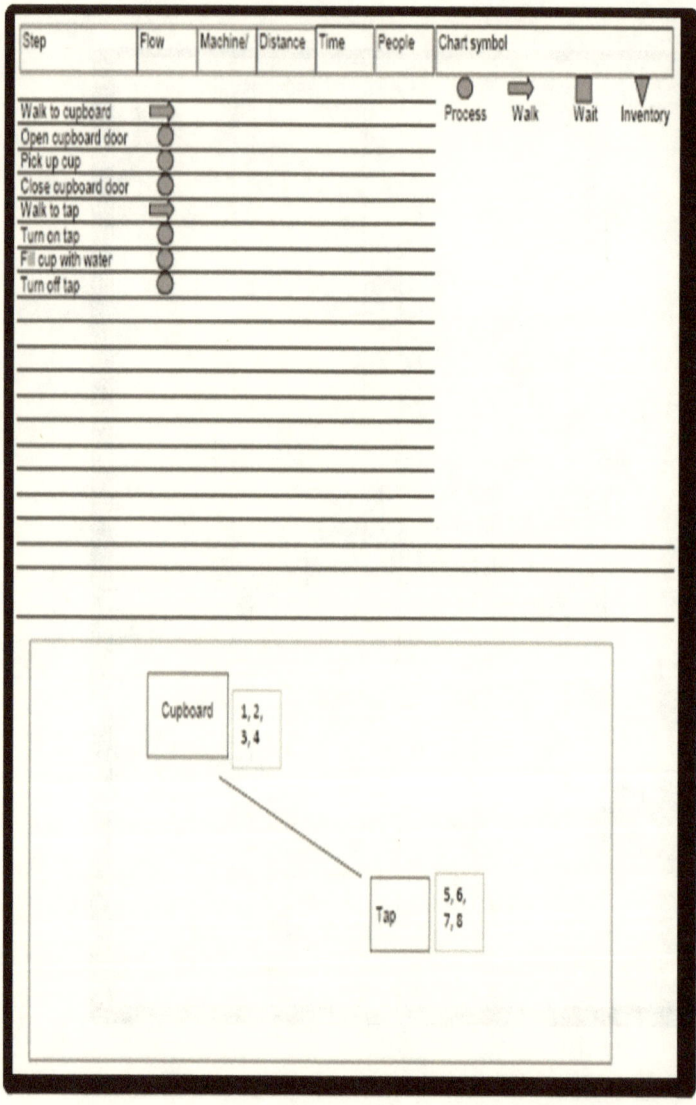

www.ingramcontent.com/pod-product-compliance
Lightning Source LLC
Chambersburg PA
CBHW021959170526
45157CB00003B/1055